RETIREMENT
OF STEEL

RETIREMENT OF STEEL

By Mitch Lyons

Dedication

I dedicate this book to my wife Angela, my best friend and biggest supporter. She has believed in me through it all, oftentimes more fervently than I believed in myself. She is a tireless giver who is the glue of our family.
I love you Ang!

ACKNOWLEDGMENTS

I'd like to thank Kat McFarlin for helping me navigate the process of writing this book. She made it much easier than I thought it would be. Thank you to Brett Kitchen and Ethan Kap for inspiring me to think bigger and recognize that "Different is better than better!" Thank you to my parents, Fred and Janet Lyons, for believing in me and never doubting me in my quest to reach my goals. Through it all, I always knew you loved and supported me. To my brother Fred, who constantly challenged me to be better. To the MANY coaches who impacted my life through the selfless giving of their time and talents. Special thanks to Dave Sukup, George Perles, and Bill Cowher, head coaches who taught me what a leader looks like. To my tight end coach in Pittsburgh, Mike Mularkey (who himself would be an NFL head coach with the Bills, Jaguars, and Titans), who made the game fun again for me after a frustrating period of time in Atlanta. Lastly, to the many clients, most of whom I consider friends as well, who entrust me to help them navigate their financial journey to a Retirement of Steel!

ABOUT THE AUTHOR

Mitch Lyons has over 20 years of experience in the financial industry. Over time he began to seriously doubt whether the "rules of thumb" and riding the Wall Street rollercoaster were really the best way to a fruitful retirement. He has since focused his efforts on educating clients about those fallacies and helping them protect their wealth from unnecessary taxes, fees, and risk.

Mitch and his wife, Angela, have a blended family with six children. They reside in Rockford, Michigan, where Mitch enjoys coaching, golf, working out, hunting, fishing, and time with family and friends at their northern Michigan cottage.

FOREWORD

Over my 33-year career in the NFL, I had the privilege to play and coach with and against some of the toughest, well prepared players of all time. Ronnie Lott, Dave Casper, Chris Doleman, Randall McDaniel, Greg Lloyd, Rod Woodson, and Dermontti Dawson were some of my teammates over my 9-year playing career. Lyle Alzado, Ted Hendricks, Reggie White, Lawrence Taylor, Mike Singletary, Hines Ward, Mark Bruener, and John Randle were some of the toughest players I was able to coach or face on Sunday afternoons.

Observing and sharing the field with such giants of the game helped me develop a profile of what it took to succeed in the brutally physical business of professional football. I could fill a couple of pages in this book from lessons I learned from them. However, one particular player during my coaching career taught me more about what toughness and what being a pro is really about. Mitch Lyons was on the offense of the Atlanta Falcons.

There was not a lot of tape on Mitch to truly evaluate his talent fairly, but one thing that stood out to me was his physical play and effort. Those are two traits that players have complete control over, and these were traits that I demanded from my position group. It was a no brainer for us to sign Mitch to be the bookend tight end with Mark Bruener.

I first met Mitch Lyons in 1997 when I was coaching the tight ends for the Pittsburgh Steelers. Mitch was a tight end who had played his college ball at Michigan State and was looking for a new home after spending 4 years playing a run & shoot offense for the Falcons. From 1997 through midway of the 1999 season, Mitch Lyons and Mark Bruener were the most physically feared pair of tight ends in the NFL.

I believe Mitch Lyons is one of the most physical blocking tight ends in NFL history, and for me, was the most enjoyable player to coach and watch perform. Unfortunately, during the 1999 season, in a game against the Chiefs in Kansas City, I lost both tight ends to knee injuries. Bruener for the season, Mitch for his career. It was one of the most emotionally upsetting games in my 24-years of coaching.

Mitch Lyons is a fierce competitor, a man of faith, and a leader who elevates the people around him. I believe you will see in the following pages in this book, that Mitch still prepares, attacks, and executes in the financial world as he did in an NFL career that was cut way too short.

- Mike Mularkey, Mitch's position coach
in Pittsburgh '97-99. Later head coach of the Buffalo
Bills, Jacksonville Jaguars and Tennessee Titans.

TABLE OF CONTENTS

CHAPTER 1

Seven Years in the NFL One Day, One Second, it's Gone

Life changes on a dime. We've seen that recently with the Covid-19 pandemic, which has redefined how we live our lives. We have also seen how one event has a ripple effect that can impact our lives profoundly. The virus that swept through the world caused more than physical illness and death. Some of its by-products hit us financially. Markets tanked, businesses closed, and people lost their jobs. Still, in the wake of the first wave of the pandemic, our nation reeled. It now braces for what comes next.

When I was born, it was also a volatile time in our country. I grew up in Michigan in a middle-class family with its share of economic trials and went through the ups and downs of the 1970s.

In many ways, my birth year was a year of extraordinary things. The Beatles officially broke up after a huge career together. The Apollo 13 mission suffered an accident on the way to the moon. In the Super Bowl that year, the

Kansas City Chiefs ran over the Minnesota Vikings and beat them 23-7.

Looking back at the time, we can see how inflation and the economy have changed so dramatically. The average rent was $140 per month. Gasoline was 36 cents per gallon.[1] An average house in the U.S. sold for $23,450! That's hardly a decent down payment today. The average household income at that time was $9,400.

In looking at prices today and comparing them to the 1970's it was hard to fathom that my family had such economic hardships given the cost of living back then. Yet, times were particularly tough not only for my family but also for many people. The country was in upheaval with the Vietnam War. Volatility was the word that best described the decade and was the backdrop for my childhood.

I grew up in my older brother's shadow. He was four years older than me. We were highly competitive, especially in athletics. Due to the age and size difference,

1   http://www.thepeoplehistory.com/1970.html#:~:text=In%20April%20of%201970%2C%20Nixon,US%20and%20South%20Vietnamese%20troops.&text=People%20stage%20massive%20protests%20against,University%20and%20Jackson%20State%20University.

I really pushed myself to compete against him. Brothers being what they are, we never missed the opportunity to compete.

The continual competition made us better. It definitely inspired me to be better and fostered a strong work ethic when it came to life, especially sports. I wanted to be like him, and naturally, I wanted to beat him in sports when I could.

Sports were a good diversion for me. I played and excelled in most sports, but football was my favorite. My dream was to play professionally. Sports were a terrific way to focus on something other than my family's financial situation. We hit some hard times during my middle school and high school years.

To make things worse, when we moved to Grand Rapids when I was in 7th grade, we rented a home in a school district where the families seemed to me to be better off than mine financially. My family was barely getting by at times. I felt a little out of place, and it was painful at that age. In my mind, the other kids were in the top tier, and I felt like I was at the bottom.

My family had several bumps in the road during that time; some of those bumps proved embarrassing for me, unreliable vehicles, and other things that made me feel insecure. Consequently, I was especially aware of my economic status. I was determined to change things so that my life would be different.

I was motivated to earn money growing up, so I would sell vegetables from our garden or do odd jobs. When I finally hit sixteen, I immediately got a real job! I got a whopping $3.35 per hour washing dishes and bussing tables at the Red-Hot Inn! I also bought my first car, a 1971 Plymouth Valiant that I purchased with my own $225! I even paid for my own car insurance. So, I was keenly aware of the tax deductions and expenses that went with life. I worked forty hours per week that summer until football started.

After football season began, I didn't have a regular job. However, I would still work to earn a few dollars when I could. One of my coaches wanted me to help clean his elderly mother's home. I did it gladly every weekend. I was frugal with my money and didn't spend it on frivolities.

As a freshman in high school, we were in the heart of economic woes. My brother graduated and was working his way through junior college. I was determined to go to college too, but it dawned on me that I may not be able to make it to college with our financial problems. I had no clue about financial aid and had no idea how it worked. Not wanting to give up my dream to go to college, I knew that I would need a scholarship, either through athletics or academics, if college was ever going to be in the picture. I was unwavering in the pursuit of my goal. At that point, though, I was all-in on football.

As a kid, I played baseball, but football and basketball were my sports of choice when I got into high school. However, football was my passion. I played quarterback at the start of my freshman year but moved to tight end. I also played linebacker and other positions during high school. I gained a lot of experience and loved every moment of it.

I did well in football. By my senior year, my hard work was rewarded when some major universities recruited me. My dream was coming true, at least I hoped so. Things looked quite promising for me. A shot at going to a great university and playing football was what I wanted most.

While I tended to root for Michigan State (mostly to oppose my brother who liked Michigan), as a kid from Michigan, you grew up in awe of the football program at the University of Michigan. Historically, it was a great program led by Bo Schembechler, who was in his 19th season as head coach at that time.

You can imagine my surprise when Coach Schembechler sat down next to me in his office, put his arm around me, and said, "Son, you owe it to yourself to be a Michigan man!" I left that meeting thinking I would be just that, a Michigan man!

Still, I was an impressionable youth, and when the University of Colorado courted me and flew me out to meet with the coaching staff, suddenly, I wanted to become a Buffalo. My decision process was still swirling. George Perles, the head coach of the Michigan State Spartans, showed considerable interest in me. The Spartans had won the 1988 Rose Bowl that season and my older brother was now attending MSU despite his earlier allegiance to U of M. Ultimately, I decided to become a Spartan with no regrets.

My freshman year was a tough time family-wise. With the addition of more economic stress, my parents ended up divorcing. Getting a job during school was out of the question because of the NCAA rules. I had to work through summers and even got some odd jobs during spring break. While other kids took off for Florida to party, I was typically working at Honey Baked Hams on the production line for Easter hams.

My college career started slowly, but I ended up starting at tight end my last two seasons. As graduation approached, the NFL Draft was on the horizon. I can't tell you how much I wanted to play professional football, and now it was a possibility! I waited by the phone, my nerves getting the better of me. Everything I ever wanted to do was wrapped up in the draft.

On the night of the first day of the draft, I got a call from the Vikings' tight end coach, Brian Billick (who later would lead the Baltimore Ravens to a Super Bowl win). He said they were looking to take me in the fifth round of the draft, and if they didn't take me then, they were going take me with their next pick. The Vikings didn't take me with their fifth-round pick, but, in the sixth round, the Atlanta Falcons selected me with the 151st pick overall before the Vikings had a shot. I was going to be a pro football player!

Dreams do come true. So, that summer, I packed up and headed off to the big city of Atlanta. It was one of the hottest summers on record, a heck of a time to go through two-a-days in full pads! Still, I was a pro football player! Jerry Glanville was the head coach. It was an overwhelming experience for me. Being on the same team with guys I watched on TV like Deion Sanders, Andre Rison, and Bobby Hebert — the heroes of the gridiron — was amazing. I was the new kid on the block and was star-struck, but I had a job to do.

Although I had a good chance of sticking with the team and playing, there were no guarantees. That's true in everything. We have what we have at that moment. Eventually, I learned I could play with those guys and that I belonged there. It was a great feeling and a sense of accomplishment. How blessed I was to have a job I loved and the career I dreamed of most of my life. Even still, I felt like there was a void in my life. In my rookie year, through the benefit of seeds planted and cultivated by some very special people over my lifetime, I accepted Jesus Christ as my savior. My life now made more sense despite the ups and downs of the NFL and life in general.

While I played quite a bit as a rookie, head coach Jerry Glanville was fired after my first season. The new coach,

June Jones, brought in his style of offense, the "Run n Shoot," which didn't utilize a tight end much. Frustration set in. Then I realized that I had to take a step back and look at the situation through my ten-year-old eyes and appreciate where I was and how far I had come. Perspective is a good thing!

I never took for granted that I would be on the team the next season. Looking at my bank balance, what I had, and what I could spend, I was cautious and prudent. I didn't let the glamour of the NFL go to my head like some other players. Many of them went out and bought a ton of stuff, never considering that things might change in an instant. The lessons I learned from my family situation made me extremely cautious with money.

Financially, I went through every year in the NFL planning as if it were my last. For all I knew, it could be, and eventually, I knew I would be right. That puts things in a different perspective, and you assume that everything will be fine. A career can be over as quickly as it began. That time almost came after my 4th season in Atlanta when June Jones was fired. The new coach, Dan Reeves, didn't re-sign me. Still, blessings were on the horizon when the Pittsburgh Steelers signed me! What a thrill that was!

It was a tumultuous time for us. My wife was pregnant with our second son, whom we had learned had heart problems during the fifth month of pregnancy. With the impending birth of my son coming in May, it was a blessing when a turbulent offseason ended with Pittsburgh signing me to a contract in April. Just in time!

The Steelers were wonderful in accommodating me with my son's situation, which would require three open-heart surgeries over his first 2 ½ years. I was happy to be on the team.

I got to play for Bill Cowher, the amazing head coach who had a tremendous run at Pittsburgh. He had been a player before coaching, and he knew what players went through. He was a consummate competitor. Bill had been a linebacker and a special teams player, so he understood the toll a player's body endures during an NFL season.

Besides playing tight end, I was also on the kickoff return team, the most dangerous team you could be on. Normally, I was in the wedge, and as such, we were targeted. When the team needs you, you don't want to say no. You want to help and to play as much as possible.

In the 14th game of the 1999 season, we were playing in Kansas City. On a late game kickoff return, I willingly went out there and did my job. The football was squib kicked to me, and off I ran. I didn't see a guy coming at me from the edge, and he hit me right in the knee. At that moment, I knew my career was over. There would be no next season. That was it!

In a split second, after seven years in the NFL, my career was over. My dream came to an end on the field of Arrowhead Stadium in Kansas City in December of 1999. I was twenty-nine. In the blink of an eye, my life was upended.

I remember recovering from surgery in January, sitting on the couch. The stock market went through a precipitous rise. I looked at my accounts and thought we'd be good to go. We'd make it through until I could find other work. As we've seen, the stock market is unpredictable. Initially, I thought we were in good shape, but the tech bubble burst, and we lost a lot of money. Just like football, the market took a big hit, and it would be a while before it recovered. Historically, the market can take years to recover. The big crash in October of 1929 proved that point, and we saw it again in 2000 and would later experience it in 2008 and 2020. Like a lot of other people, I lost money when the bubble burst, leaving a void. Money lost is lost. Brokers can spin it dozens of ways, but money was lost. It's like the win/loss column in football. You don't get to undo your losses and turn them into wins.

There are no two ways around it. The years 2000, 2001, and 2002 were tough times for the stock market. It was also a rough time beginning my life after football as a financial advisor. Due to 9-11, people wanted to hang on to their money. I understood that. You want to be in control and should be in control of your money. After coming off some big lessons that reinforced the need to have control, I wanted to change things not only for me but for my clients.

Something better had to be out there to help us save for our retirement and have control over our money. You work too hard not to have control over your money. We all do. No one wants to take a big financial hit.

Things started to turn around, and like others, I put my money in the market only to take another big hit in 2008. The country reeled as we watched our accounts get sacked by the financial crisis. The thing was you didn't see a referee toss a flag. There were no real penalties on the broker side of things. It was the clients who took the hit. Talk about unnecessary roughness!

We were told to hang in there and to keep the rest of our money in the market. Of course, brokers would say that because that's how they make their money. I had had enough, though, and knew there was something better out there.

Let's face it. If you lose 20 percent of your money, you're going to have to get a 25 percent rebound just to break even. Meanwhile, you've lost time and money. All the fuzzy math in the world can't hide the loss. It's not just a loss on paper. It's the real deal. It's your money.

The volatility in the market highlights the gamble we take when we invest our money in the market. The risk is much the same as it is in casinos. I don't know about you, but gambling with my money doesn't give me a sense of security.

After two big blows in the market, I knew I didn't want to give my clients the bad news when the market tanks again. I couldn't look them in the eye in good conscience and recommend putting their funds in stocks, knowing full well that the market could and would tank again.

As we've seen with the Covid-19 financial reaction, the market was hyper-reactive. With the soft economy, things are looking dismal for many investors who were in the market or who have stayed in hoping to recoup their losses. Many people suffered a 40 percent loss in 2008. Can you really afford to take a hit that big? Not many of us can.

If you look at retirement logically, evaluate where you want to be, and define your goals, you can create a positive game plan to cross the goal line.

> **Can you make money without the market and avoid getting run over by a raging bull?**

Yes!

I have done that. I changed my playbook and learned the nuances of indexing. I don't need to worry about losses. The game plan has a strong defense to protect your wealth and a potent offense to grow your wealth. I'll show you how that works.

You don't need to worry about the stock market ticker, wondering when stocks are going to bounce back. There is a positive and secure way to grow your wealth. I'll teach you the Mitch Lyons Wealth System, where you can grow your money securely. If you're ready to change your life and grow your wealth, then let's go!

CHAPTER 2

Tackling Taxes in Retirement

Life in the NFL was hectic. Being new to the league, I carved out my career and tried to be the best player I could. Football is a tough sport, and the day-to-day can be grueling. It goes without saying that it's not the normal 9 to 5 job. The average career lasts just over three years.

While we not only had our daily routine, there was also a lot of travel involved. There was a lot to handle from learning assignments and keeping up with game films and training. A lot of the players had wives and kids. I was no exception. Certainly, that added to the To-Do list.

By my fourth year in the league, my wife was pregnant with our second child. We were looking forward to our new addition!

Expecting a child is like waiting for Christmas. Preparations need to be made. Those nine months can be extremely busy. You wonder what sex the baby will be, and then you debate with your spouse if you want to know ahead of time. No one anticipates anything out of the ordinary. You conceive, you go through the gestation period, and then the baby arrives. Simple, right?

The Falcons were preparing for our last game of the season, an away game at Jacksonville to finish up the lackluster 1996 season at 3-13. My wife had already left Atlanta and returned home to Michigan.

She had an unscheduled ultrasound on her last visit with her doctor before leaving Atlanta, and things looked okay. The doctor just snuck in the ultrasound to check the sex of the baby. My wife had already scheduled one to be done when she got home for grandparents to be a part of. We discovered that the baby was a boy! However, they didn't look at everything that closely as they were just taking a quick look to find out about the gender.

After getting back to Michigan, my wife kept the appointment for the second ultrasound so our moms could go with her and see the baby. It was truly a happy time. It was during that ultrasound that it was determined our son had an issue with his heart. The heart wasn't developing correctly. From the heights of happiness to the discovery of a serious and life-threatening condition, my wife got hit with the bad news.

I was out on the practice field, focusing on the upcoming game. The equipment manager came running out and headed straight for me. It was unusual, and my gut told me something was wrong. He told me I had a call that I needed to take. Immediately, my stomach lurched. It wasn't a good feeling. They don't pull you out of practice for no reason. I knew something serious had happened. The look on the manager's face was somber.

I ran to the phone and got the news. Our son was diagnosed with a hypoplastic left heart, an uncommon congenital defect that involves the improper formation of one side of the heart. Basically, he only had one ventricle able to pump blood, as opposed to two. The news was horrible.

To correct the situation after he was delivered, he would have to endure a process that would include three open-heart surgeries. The first surgery was to take place as soon as possible.

We initially were going to have the surgery done at the University of Michigan, but the heart surgeon there was at a medical conference in Hawaii and then planned on staying another week in the islands. Since time was of the essence, we had to find someone else.

Dr. Roger Mee at the Cleveland Clinic was world-renowned and, by the grace of God, available. Our little guy, who had been in the hospital about a week in Grand Rapids, was taken by helicopter to Cleveland, and we followed by car. It was a tough time. Not knowing how things would work out was awful, but we had to trust in the Lord. He had his first open-heart surgery and stayed at the clinic for about ten days.

Our son did all right, but we knew he still needed the two additional surgeries. At three months old, he was back for another surgery. It was like living on pins and needles. The process consisted of rewiring his heart so he could live with his one functioning ventricle.

Normal hearts pump blood to the lungs where it receives oxygen and then back to the heart to be pumped back out to the body. In our son's case, his heart was rewired to pump blood out to the body and then return passively to the lungs. As you can imagine, it's a delicate surgery. Basically, they tie the superior and inferior vena cava into the lungs. I got to know a great deal about the condition and way more about the heart than I ever would have liked.

He weathered that surgery just fine. When he got older, he had the third surgery done. Getting right down to it, we had a perfectly healthy boy one minute, and the next minute we discovered he had a life-threatening illness.

At the first surgery, we were told that the mortality rate was 15 percent giving the baby an 85 percent chance of making it. Those odds looked good, and I'd take those odds any day, except for one thing. When it's your child's life you're betting on, those odds aren't good at all.

Let me tell you, we ran the gamut of emotions, and it was hard to express what we felt. A nurse at the Cleveland Clinic articulated it succinctly when she told us we were mourning the loss of a healthy child. We fully expected to have a healthy baby, and suddenly that was not the case. It took time to adjust. She told us that our second son would never be a perfectly healthy child. Those were sober words to hear, and it was difficult to live with that knowledge.

As he grew, he couldn't play sports that required heavy cardiovascular strength, but he could play Little League as he got a little older, and that was special given his love of sports.

However, our son is doing fine now. He's twenty-three, and you wouldn't really know anything was wrong with him. He plays some golf and is currently a graduate assistant at Michigan State on the women's basketball program. We don't know what the future holds, but we'll get through it each day, trusting in the Lord.

Taxes are remarkably similar to our son's situation. As we near retirement, it's like the gestational period of pregnancy. The possibilities and the enthusiasm grow as we get closer to our retirement date, just like a due date.

Like expecting a baby, retirement takes planning and care. Naturally, we want everything to go well. So, we make sure that we invest wisely and plan for any contingencies. We know that taxes come due at a certain time each year. Our incomes fuel the taxation process, and then when it comes time to find out our tax debt, we sit down and discover how much we're going to pay.

Given the current climate in the country and the world today, none of us can predict what tax bracket we will be in from one year to the next. Things are in flux. Things can change, as they did with my son. You expect something to be okay, and then you're hit with the unexpected.

It would be prudent to anticipate that you will be bear a higher tax burden in future years. Lately, we have seen that tax brackets have been the same in 2019 and 2020.[2]

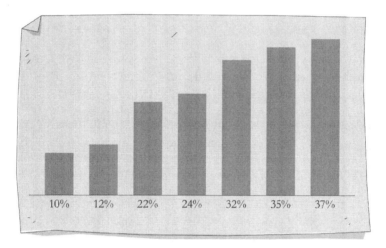

| 10% | 12% | 22% | 24% | 32% | 35% | 37% |

The tax brackets haven't changed, but the tax bracket *ranges* have, resulting in many people ending up in a different bracket, even though their incomes didn't rise.

With the likelihood that tax ranges and brackets will continue to change as we continue through our current financial situation in this country, it's important to

2   https://www.kiplinger.com/article/taxes/t056-c000-s001-what-are-the-income-tax-brackets-for-2020-vs-2019.html

prepare for those changes. None of us has a crystal ball that helps us to predict our future needs nor tax obligations. Nevertheless, we can determine our income streams, where they are coming from, and how long they will last.

Most people have built up their Social Security for their retirement. It's automatic.

Did you know that Social Security will no longer be fully funded in 2034?

It will only be funded approximately 75 percent. [3]

That's a disconcerting statistic given that most Americans over the age of sixty currently rely only on Social Security for retirement income!

---

3   https://blog.ssa.gov/social-security-funded-until-2034-and-about-three-quarters-funded-for-the-long-term-many-options-to-address-the-long-term-shortfall/

Do you know what your Social Security benefit will be?

Most people really don't know what they'll be getting. They haven't put pen to paper to figure it out. Will your Social Security income be enough to allow you to live the lifestyle you desire and still pay your taxes?

The chances are good that adjustments to your lifestyle will need to be made. People typically haven't dug down to ascertain what income they will be receiving and if it will meet their needs. Finding out where you stand sooner rather than later is important. It's imperative to have strong financial strategies in place to handle the unexpected.

We have witnessed lately that the economy can be upended quickly. The Covid-19 crisis affirmed that. It's been my experience that the amount clients believed they'd need to pay for retirement expenses, isn't the number they'll draw out of their retirement accounts. Therefore, it's hard to pin down the tax bracket.

Don't let the disparity between what you need to pay for expenses and taxes and what you'll get tackle your retirement plans.

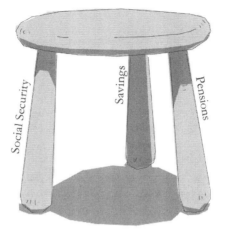

Unless you win the lottery, most retirement income comes from three sources. The figure above demonstrates the theory of the *Three-Legged Stool,* comprised of Social Security, pensions, and savings. However, a recent study showed that just 6.8 percent of Americans over 60 years old, who work under thirty hours per week, are, actually, getting income from Social Security, pensions (also called Defined Benefit Plans), and savings like 401ks.[4]

---

4   https://www.cnbc.com/2020/01/17/heres-where-most-ameri-cans-are-really-getting-their-retirement-income.html

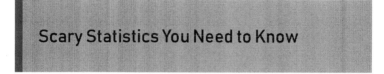

Scary Statistics You Need to Know

To better emphasize the need for proper retirement planning, look at these statistics:

GoBankingRates.com listed some startling facts from a recent survey. Of those responding to the survey, about 45 percent of Americans have *Zero* dollars in savings. Those polled stated the reason they have no savings is that they are living from paycheck to paycheck.

Another alarming statistic the poll revealed is that 69 percent of Americans have less than $1000 saved![5]

Obviously, these figures are a testimony to the world-wide turbulence of late. The stimulus checks issued during the Covid-19 crisis were necessary to keep the country going forward. The problem lies in the fact that the amount of money that funded those checks, along with other social programs needs to be repaid. Raising taxes or changing tax bracket standards will probably come into play. There is no such thing as a free lunch!

5   https://www.gobankingrates.com/saving-money/savings-advice/americans-have-less-than-1000-in-savings/

Despite changes in the world economy, we will be faced with retirement and trying to fund it. I mentioned earlier that it is important to diversify your retirement income and offset your taxes by getting as much tax-free income as possible.

The growing trends we see today indicate that you must be prepared to handle the unexpected that may come along and attack your retirement income.

I was hit with unexpected taxes while playing in the NFL. I soon discovered that my paycheck had more taxes taken out. I thought if you got paid in Georgia (Falcons) or Pennsylvania (Steelers), those would be the only state tax obligations I had. Wrong! I had to pay state tax in every state where I "played." That meant filing returns for each state! Who knew?

> **Taxes are a certainty. What is uncertain is how much tax will you have to pay?**

Even if you can stay in your current tax bracket, deductions may change dramatically, affecting the bottom line on your 1040! If they lower the threshold on tax brackets or remove deductions, that's money coming out of *your* pocket!

Today, we have any number of taxes that take money out of our pockets. Taxes such as sales, property, gasoline, estate, personal and federal taxes, along with the capital gains tax and a bevy of others, should remind us that we need to build a fortress to protect our incomes from unnecessary taxes. Even 401ks are subject to taxes, as are other investments.

Hidden fees, interest rates, and other fees add to your financial burden and dim the brightness of your retirement. Making sound decisions for your retirement is crucial if you are going to maintain your lifestyle and enjoy retirement.

Legally lowering your taxes is an important step. For instance, if you have money in a 401k, you may be getting matching funds and not paying taxes on the income used to fund that account. However, the time will come when you need to withdraw funds out of necessity or by requirement. That money is taxable. It's a certainty. So, let's look at how you can pay fewer taxes and shift some of those funds into a guaranteed tax-free income.

If you were to plant a field of corn, you would need to buy seed. If, when you went to the store to buy the seed, the store owner gave you the chance to pay tax on the seed now or pay after the harvest, it may be enticing to pay later. However, if you pay for the seed now, you will pay much less than if you had to pay tax on the entire harvest!

Your 401k is like that. If you could move your money into a more fertile field, where it isn't exposed to the elements like financial hail, floods, or drought, wouldn't that be the smart thing to do? Absolutely!

The key is to lower your tax exposure legally by placing your money where it is safe, where it will grow and where it can be withdrawn without being taxed. Financial vehicles like Indexed Universal Life (IUL) contracts can provide a tax-free retirement income option when structured properly.

Limiting your tax exposure puts more money in your pocket. By taking the necessary steps now, you can mitigate taxes and allow for cost of living adjustments. Using a professionally designed IUL can really be a game-changer. We will take a deeper dive into the benefits that an IUL can provide later.

Often when we are hit with financial shake-ups, a ripple effect occurs. When we found out our son would be born with medical issues, a ripple effect of events followed his delivery. It changed his life and ours. Preparing for the unexpected is pivotal in retirement.

Many people are choosing to delay retirement because they don't think they can afford to retire. Others go back to work part-time while drawing Social Security. That can bring about more taxes and can affect your Social Security check.

Knowing what to expect and how to handle your expenses ahead of time is beneficial in having a healthy and happy retirement. Flexibility in your retirement plan will help you keep taxes under control and still provide for the unexpected. Finding the right investment vehicle will ensure that you are protected.

I can help you find the right vehicle, one that is properly structured to protect your money today and in the future. Taxes will always be in our lives, but if we plan how to combat them legally, you won't be taken out of the game.

In life and even in death, we are taxed. In fact, if you make money, you WILL be taxed. If you spend money, you WILL be taxed. When you die, you guessed it; you WILL be taxed!

Much like using the right strategy to win a football game, if you utilize proper financial tools, they will help you to succeed.

Don't worry! You aren't alone. I'll coach you every step of the way! It's my job, one that I take seriously. Proper planning and growing your wealth through well-designed vehicles like IULs and others can lessen your tax burden.

In the next chapter, we'll look at other expenses that can eat away at your retirement. Are you ready to protect your assets? Let's find out how!

CHAPTER 3

Health Care and Donut Holes

During all my years of playing football, the word "concussion" wasn't really used. Sure, we talked about getting "clocked," getting your "bell rung," and "seeing stars," but "concussion" wasn't in the vernacular of NFL Locker rooms. Yes, I did see stars and had my bell rung on more than one occasion. It's not something we thought about much. Getting hit and occasionally feeling woozy were things that went with playing football. We were tough guys and didn't think much of it.

Now we know that concussions are quite prevalent in the game, and we now have a better understanding of the potential long-term effects. The NFL took notice and finally became proactive. Certainly, that is to the benefit of all the players. We've seen lots of players who have had severe concussions. Gradually, the NFL realized that players needed to be protected, and parameters needed to be put into place to ensure each player's safety.

When I saw stars, I just went back into the game. I never wanted to give up my role on the team, even for a couple of plays, for fear that I might not get it back. For me, I thought it was better to keep playing than to admit that my mind was a bit foggy. As awareness of the ramifications of concussions and their potential long-term effects have become more known, players certainly have more to think about now.

In 2017, the NFL reached an agreement on the Concussion Settlement that would benefit players who suffered brain injuries while playing football for the league. Mike Webster, a former Pittsburgh Steeler, died in 2002. An autopsy found that Mike died of CTE, Chronic Traumatic Encephalopathy. Junior Seau, a San Diego Charger great, committed suicide and his autopsy revealed he also had CTE. The movie "Concussion," starring Will Smith, covered the problems players face with concussions and brain injuries.

I played with Justin Strzelczyk, whose story was highlighted in the film "Concussion." (An interesting side note — Justin's character was played by Matt Willig, who was my teammate in Atlanta before becoming an actor after his NFL career.) Justin was an offensive lineman, and we hung around together for about three years. Justin was a great guy and fun to be around. Six years after he quit playing, Justin started having mental health issues.

He began acting strangely. He was in a bizarre frame of mind when he went to a gas station. Justin was talking wildly and asking people strange questions. Clearly, he wasn't his usual self.

He drove away from the gas station at a high rate of speed. The police ended up following him. Ultimately, he went the wrong way on a highway and hit a tanker truck. It was a horrible, tragic death that rocked everyone who knew him and the community at large. At thirty-six, my friend was dead. An autopsy revealed he had brain injuries related to his playing days.

Shane Dronett played for the Falcons when I was in Atlanta. He had a good career going and just signed a $20 million contract with the Falcons. He ended up tearing his ACL, and things started to get worse for him. Shane's family noticed that he was exhibiting strange behavior. They had him checked out and found that he had a benign tumor in his brain. It was removed, but his behavior didn't improve. He continued down a wrong path and eventually shot himself. He also was found to have CTE from doing what he loved to do, playing football.

Knowing these players and having suffered some significant hits myself, I'm careful about my health. I've had no issues thus far, and I have had cognitive testing done to provide a reference point for down the road. Knowing what we know now about brain health, I'm quite thankful that I didn't get as much playing time as I might have liked over the years! As I've gotten older, I've become much more conscious of my overall health and the importance of staying on top of it.

Having health coverage is especially important not only now but also during retirement. The older you live, the more likely it is that you'll need medical care. No one really plans to get sick, but it happens.

> **People who don't have coverage are at greater risk because they don't seek medical care, even though they may need it.**

The lack of health insurance can create a snowball effect that puts your health in jeopardy.

The cost of medical care is quite high. Offsetting those costs by having health care insurance provides a financial buffer for your family. Sometimes, though, it's not enough.

Predicting health care costs is difficult. Some analysts believe you can use historical medical data for each patient to get some idea of future expenses. Since medical costs continue to rise, those predictions may not adequately provide accurate treatment cost predictions.[6]

Statistics show that in 2017, some 28 million Americans or 8.8 percent of the population did not have health care coverage.[7]

That percentage is likely higher today since many people lost their jobs and, as a result, their health insurance during the Covid-19 outbreak. It is estimated that some 27 million people could be left without insurance because of the fallout during the virus crisis.[8]

Even those who were insured and contracted the virus and were hospitalized found significant gaps in their coverage.

---

6   https://www.liebertpub.com/doi/full/10.1089/big.2018.0096

7   https://www.census.gov/library/publications/2018/demo/p60-264.html

8   https://www.ama-assn.org/delivering-care/patient-support-advocacy/
covid-19-job-loss-could-leave-27-million-uninsured-what-do

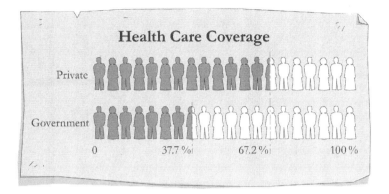

The number of people aged 65 or older and on Medicare is estimated at 58.6 percent or approximately 17.8 percent of the population.[9]

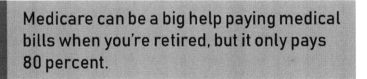

Medicare can be a big help paying medical bills when you're retired, but it only pays 80 percent.

Unless you have supplemental insurance, you will be responsible for the remaining 20 percent of total costs. Should you not have supplemental insurance, will your retirement income be enough to handle those additional out of pocket expenses?

---

9   https://www.statista.com/statistics/200962/percentage-of-ameri-cans-covered-by-medicare/

When figuring your retirement needs and income, you'll need to plan to meet your expenses, but it's also important to consider prescription costs. If you are on Medicare and have Part D for prescriptions, you need to learn about the "donut hole" that exists and how it will impact your bottom line.

The donut hole is reached when you and your Medicare coverage have paid a certain amount for prescriptions in any given year. The donut hole amount for 2020 is $4020.

That means you will be responsible for paying up to 25% of your prescription costs for brand-name prescription drugs. The gap in full-coverage will end once your out-of-pocket covered drug expenses plus a 5% plan coverage and what the manufacturer pays (70% of the cost of the drug) hits $6,350. Then you're out of the donut hole.[10]

It can appear complicated, but if you do your homework, you'll be better prepared. You'll get a clearer picture of how important it is to plan for retirement.

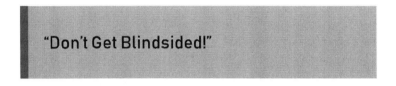

"Don't Get Blindsided!"

You don't want to be like a quarterback standing in the pocket too long, trying to throw a pass to covered receivers. You may be so focused that you do not realize you're about to be blindsided by unexpected costs.

LONG TERM CARE

Longevity can have its advantages. If you're blessed with good genes and health, you could easily live long enough to enjoy your grandchildren and maybe even your great-

---

10   https://www.65incorporated.com/topics/medicare-part-d-prescription-drug-plans/medicare-donut-hole-closing/
And:https://www.medicare.gov/drug-coverage-part-d/costs-for-medicare-drug-coverage/costs-in-the-coverage-gap

grandchildren. The problem with living longer is that the chances that you will need long-term care will increase.

> **When you reach 65 or older, your chance for needing long-term care is about 70 percent!**

According to Termcare.gov, women's average need for long-term care is listed at 3.7 years compared to men who need it for 2.2 years. While 33% of those over 65 never need long-term care, 20 percent of those who do need for an average of 5 years.[11]

In long-term care facilities, a semi-private room averages about $6844 per month, and a private room costs about $7698! Whether you're a man or woman, that's a great deal of money that you'll need to cover. Having long-term care coverage helps. It's critical to look at your portfolio and your monthly retirement income to determine if you can pay for long-term care.

There are significant side-effects when it comes to long-term care and not just for the patient. The spouse may

---

11   https://longtermcare.acl.gov/the-basics/how-much-care-will-you-need.html

become the designated caregiver, often forcing the spouse to give up their jobs and savings.

I was having breakfast with a friend a few years ago. He talked about his plans for the future, what he and his wife wanted to do in retirement, and talked about his kids, who were finishing college. The future looked bright for them. He looked great, and I really enjoyed seeing him and hearing his plans.

Within a month, in the blink of an eye, the man was hit by a massive stroke. He survived but was in bad shape. His life would never be the same, and neither would his family's. Everything was upended for them. The man could no longer work, and financially, he was nowhere near ready to retire. Out of necessity, his wife had to become a full-time caregiver, precluding her from working outside the home. Their plans for the future were shot.

I ran into his wife at the store not too long ago. I gave her a hug and asked how she was doing. You could tell by the look in her eyes she was exhausted.

Many people who suffer catastrophic illness and need long-term care find themselves in a quandary. Without proper planning ahead of time, one catastrophic event can turn your world upside down. You can hit the ceiling or coverage cap leaving giant financial holes. I make sure my clients are aware of vehicles that can offer protection against these types of perils and typically no additional charge. Riders can provide sound financial protection for the unexpected events life can bring when added to a policy or contract.

It's unlikely my friends could pay for long-term care, as is the case with many couples. The monthly fees are astronomical. Medicare only covers so much. Without a long-term care policy or rider, families in this situation would likely have to spend-down their assets before Medicaid would click in. The qualifications for Medicaid are specific and don't allow any wiggle room. If there are assets that can be liquidated, the family must liquidate them to qualify for long-term care. Spouses in that situation may find themselves without a place to live.

Health care is a definite concern when it comes to retirement planning. Often people just assume they have enough coverage or enough in savings. Yet, with the soaring costs of care, how much savings are really enough?

Can your savings accounts grow fast enough to stay ahead of medical costs?

It's a gamble, one where the odds are against you. We all need to do our part in offsetting health care costs. That includes taking care of ourselves, eating right, and exercising regularly. All my life, I wanted to be an athlete. I worked out from an early age. I loved it. Some days may be tougher than others, particularly when it comes to keeping our workout schedules going. If I miss a day or two, I know it. I feel it. I'd rather workout and feel better, and be better. It takes discipline but so does retirement planning.

Sure, there are one-hundred-year-old guys who smoke a pack of cigarettes every day who can run circles around us, and then there are thirty-year old's who drop dead from heart attacks. The point is, we must do our part.

As mentioned earlier, it's nearly impossible to predict where health care costs will go, but most certainly, they won't recede. It's prudent to prepare and get your retirement portfolio and health care decisions ready for your future. Establishing Health Savings Accounts can help cover out of pocket expenses and premiums should you find yourself in financial difficulty.

Indexed Universal Life offers a strong defense against rising healthcare costs, with riders allowing access to your death benefit with a chronic or critical illness diagnosis. Some annuities will double your guaranteed income under certain conditions like catastrophic illness, long-term care, cancer, and so on.

If you plan and invest ahead of time in a properly structured IUL or annuity, you can have a financial arsenal at your disposal. So, even if you lose your job and your health benefits, you'll still be able to get through the crisis in good shape. The IUL and Annuity game plan is a strong defense against the unexpected. Not only that, but you'll bridge the gap when financial blows hit, and you'll be able to weather strong storms.

Should Women Plan Differently When It Comes to Health Care?

Women live longer, normally about 81 years now, while men average about 78 years. Consequently, they will need to make sure they will not outlive their money. If an unexpected health care crisis arises and happens without sufficient coverage, a woman will have a much tougher time making ends meet should she survive the initial event. Making sure there is enough guaranteed income is vital.

I sit down with my clients and find out their needs. Knowing their family health history and whether there is longevity in their family tree helps tremendously to nail down the right approach to investing for retirement.

Health care and its unpredictability can be stressful. Financial health is directly associated with physical health. Studies have shown there is a direct correlation between physical, financial, and even psychological health.[12]

During the 2008-2010 financial crisis in our country, research was done by UCLA, Duke, and Drexel University, that reported Americans who had financial stress had higher blood pressure and higher blood glucose levels. Further, during that time period, there were increased numbers of people suffering from depression, anxiety, sleep disorders, ulcers, and other maladies.

---

12   https://www.marcus.com/us/en/resources/personal-finance/physical-and-financial-health
https://www.schwab.com/resource-center/insights/content/beyond-4-rule-how-much-can-you-safely-spend-retirement

Obviously, if those illnesses go unchecked, undiagnosed, and untreated, people may suffer further health problems. By proper planning, your retirement, and your portfolio, you're inoculating your financial health against all sorts of unforeseen maladies.

You want to be able to protect your wealth and your health the best way possible. Leaving your wealth and health exposed to a variety of problems is detrimental.

You can take control. You can take charge. If you don't have enough funds, you can go on a financial diet restricting your spending and saving all you can. Moving your assets into the right vehicles will give your money the chance to grow while it builds protection for you and your family.

Building financial and physical health and stamina requires considerate coaching. That's where I can help. Having been through the Code Blue of the financial flu, I know what it takes to resuscitate your wealth and get it into the best shape possible so that it will outlive you no matter what.

Health care costs and premiums will rise. Let me show you the steps you can take to stay ahead of the costs.

You owe it to yourself to eliminate unnecessary risks through proper financial planning that will ward off the high costs of health care.

Balance the uncertainties of life with the predictability of a guaranteed income that will provide for your needs in health and in illness. By increasing your financial strength, you will lower your stress and ward off stress-related illness.

Going over this chapter, it brings up some pertinent points about having enough money to meet your expenses and still maintain your lifestyle. Having your money outlive you is key, but there's a big question attached to that. How? Well, I'll show you in the next chapter!

CHAPTER 4

Running Out of Money!

On a hot August night, we had a preseason game in Philadelphia against our in-state rivals, the Eagles. Even though it was preseason, we took the game very seriously, as did the Eagles. Bragging rights were on the line.

I was in the lineup at tight end. The ball was snapped, and we ran our patterns. I slipped past the safety who had been fooled by the run fake, and I was in the open. The quarterback, Mike Tomczak, threw the ball and I caught it. Simple, huh? Well, it's what you do with the ball after you catch it that counts. I had two defensive players in hot pursuit, gaining ground quickly. Never a speedster, I ran for my life!

As fast as they were approaching, I knew I needed to put things in second gear. The end zone was in sight, but the guys were closing in on me. The end zone appeared even further away. It was going to be close.

I felt like an antelope trying to outrun two lions. To my surprise, I made the 61-yard run into the end zone untouched and unscathed from the defenders who pursued me. I was huffing and puffing, but I made it! That was the longest play of my career.

On the kickoff team, you really had to run hard too, but you always had to look out for blockers. We were always told to keep our heads on a swivel because blockers could come out of nowhere and blindside us. Not keeping your head on a swivel meant you could get nailed. The other team would try to knock your block off. (Rules against headhunting, were not in effect back then!) Guys crisscrossing the field were hard to see. In those fast seconds following the kickoff, you're exposed to all sorts of hazards. If you don't keep swiveling your head, you're going to get picked off.

Football and financial planning can have a lot in common.

> **You must be aware of the dangers that can literally come out of nowhere!**

Planning for retirement is a serious business. Careful planning is required to ensure that you will have enough money to live out your retirement. Working hard all your life, you've saved and planned to enjoy your retirement years. One of the key components to a happy retirement is making sure that you don't outlive your money.

Today, people are living longer. Taking good care of your nest egg is more important than ever. With longevity comes the risk that your funds will be depleted before you die.

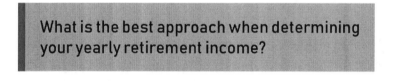

What is the best approach when determining your yearly retirement income?

Many experts feel that following the 4 Percent Rule is a prudent path to take. By adding up all your investments, then calculating 4 percent of that total establishes your yearly income. Using that guideline, it should keep you safe. For example, let's say you have saved $100.000. Applying the 4 percent rule means you would have a yearly income of $4,000. You can adjust your income in the following years to keep within that rule and adjust your income to keep up with inflation.[13]

Some experts say that the 4 Percent Rule makes a retiree scrimp, while their portfolio can often mushroom. Other experts say that even 4 percent may be too much. I've had clients tell me they would like to withdraw 7 percent per year, but that is likely excessive. The 4 Percent Rule is a general rule of thumb, but with today's low-interest-rate environment, it may be a bit too optimistic. Having adequate principal is essential along with a plan that can keep your income on pace with inflation and rising healthcare costs.

After the Covid-19 crisis, rumblings were heard about the likelihood of another Great Depression. Granted, we were still in the throes of the lockdown when some experts were drawing parallels between the lockdown and the 1929 stock market crash and the Great Depression that subsequently followed.

Anything is possible! We have seen market crashes over the years, such as the 2000 and 2008 crashes discussed

---

13   Retirement Basics: What Is The 4% Rule? – Forbes Advisor

previously. People lost significant amounts of money, putting off retirement for many.

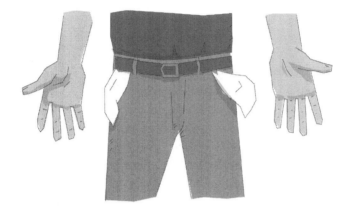

It's hard to build your wealth during economic downturns, and that may mean that you may outlive your money.

While it may be difficult to build your wealth, it is not impossible.

Retirement planning is definitely subjective. No two people are alike, nor are their portfolios. Carefully planning for your retirement should be tailor-made to meet your savings and income needs for the present and for the future.

Using the 4 Percent Rule to gauge your withdrawal rate, how can you determine if you have saved enough money to retire and not outlive those funds?

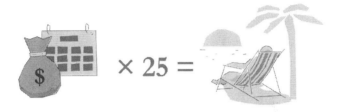

We can use the "Multiply by 25 Rule." Think about how much money you'll need each year to meet your expenses and maintain your lifestyle.

Let's say you decided that you need $40,000 per year to meet your goals. Okay. Take $40,000 and multiply it by 25. What do you need for retirement? 1 million dollars!

Since that number isn't adjusted for inflation, you need to make sure that the amount of money you withdraw will be sufficient to keep up with inflation.

We can't tell what the future will bring, but we can use data and trends to get a good idea of what we may face down the road. In calculating inflation, we usually plug in 3 percent in our retirement income calculations. Of course, inflation may vary through the years, but getting the median number and working from there will give you a good idea about inflation-proofing your income.

The best course of action is to have a game plan established *before* retirement, especially if you're still in the accumulation phase of building your wealth. I encourage my clients to take a close look at their expenses and their needs as well as their goals for retirement. If you're in the accumulation phase, you have time to adjust your savings to be better prepared for the distribution phase of retirement.

> Another point to consider is that retirees spend more in the first ten years of retirement.

This is due to the fact that a person's health is better in their sixties. Additionally, the first ten years of retirement is normally the time for people to live out the dreams they have saved for their entire working life.

Many people want to travel while they can and do things they couldn't do while working. Going on dream vacations, doing things they've dreamed about for years can come with high price tags. Those early years and the euphoria a person feels may cloud the reality of what a person can afford to do and still have enough money until they die. After you retire, expenses may change. Often, expenses can go down, but on the other hand, some expenses increase. Take healthcare, for instance, which is much more likely to be utilized as you age.

We don't know if Social Security will always be there. It may look entirely different in the coming years. At my age, there are no guarantees that I'll ever see a dime from Social Security by the time I hit retirement. It's my philosophy to plan as though Social Security will not be there. Even if it is, it will probably look different than the current model. I'm taking a conservative approach to my retirement planning, and I advise my clients to do the same.

> "I would much rather see my clients have a surplus of money at the end of their lives than to have them go through a big chunk of it in the early years of retirement."

Spending a good deal of your wealth in those early years is like running down the field with a football carried too loosely. Your teammates may miss their blocks and fail to protect you, and you're left with extraordinarily little help. Getting tackled with unexpected financial hits may cause you to fumble your financial future away.

The goal of solid financial planning is to make sure you don't fumble the ball on your way to the end zone. Remember to swivel your head and look for the things in life that will strip you of your wealth.

I've had people come to me for help in their retirement planning, who had a lot of questions that needed answering. I discovered that many people don't have a clear understanding of what their income will be. They don't have a handle on the numbers and what they mean.

It's easy to make a wrong turn when you're in the dark. Clients should be given all the information available to help them make sound decisions when it comes to their future. We have heard the general rule that you will need 70 percent of your pre-retirement income in retirement. The thing is, I haven't found that to be necessarily true because each retiree is different. It's best to put pencil to paper to better understand what a person is looking at, the numbers involved, and consider possible retirement scenarios to figure things out. We've all seen football games where someone fumbles the ball, and the opposing player scoops it up only to run in the wrong direction. All his effort to outrun the opponents goes for naught when he crosses the other team's goal line! You must know where you're going at all times!

Just so you know, you're not in this alone. I can be there for you to help you create the best strategy for your money. We can work through your numbers together and develop a strong offense, along with a powerful defense against the unexpected. Working things out on paper is advantageous. You will see things in a whole new light and will have a solid idea of what to expect before you flip the switch on retirement. When you do flip the switch, you want to see things clearly and have them run smoothly throughout your retirement years!

Some of the most incredible highlight plays in football have been when running backs run down the field and are swarmed by several players. You probably have seen some remarkable running backs like Jim Brown and Earl Campbell carrying several guys on their backs while trying to gain yardage. Those backs are tenacious and do their best, but they're not always successful.

Those opponents are like debts. As you approach retirement, you want to limit your debt and lessen the load. Carrying all the extra debt can weigh you down and increase the chances that you'll get tackled.

> **Did you know it is possible to live well and not have to be too frugal in retirement?**

For many people hitting retirement, it's their first experience living on a fixed income. A fixed income may come as a shock or even a hardship for those used to salary increases and other benefits during working years. Yet, it doesn't have to be. Readjusting how you look at things will help you through the metamorphosis. Fixed income doesn't automatically mean it's a negative thing. Prudent planning can ensure that your fixed income is more than enough to see you through.

Leaving college football for the pros meant that I had to learn a new type of offense. There were new plays, cadences, and ways of doing things that seemed foreign at first. The learning curve felt like it was steep. However, after a brief adjustment period, I got used to the new environment. Just because it was different didn't make it a bad thing. The same is true in retirement.

> ## Did you know 56 percent of Americans run out of money by the end of the month?

A recent survey put out by ING indicated that over half of the population suffers from the end of the month financial woes.[14]

As I mentioned earlier, putting pencil to paper and drawing up a budget can help you stay within your monthly limits and eliminate worry. If you've never been one to budget, you're not alone. The same ING survey indicated that only 41 percent of American households keep budgets. Still, drafting a realistic budget that you put into practice will help you to live without worry.

Using a sound investment strategy provides reassurance that your money will always be there, month after month. Even if you spend all your income each month, you'll have the certainty of knowing that the checks will continue throughout your life.

Using both long and short-term strategies can also help fortify your retirement, increasing your wealth. With the

14   https://www.acorns.com/money-basics/saving-and-budgeting/budget-meaning/

right planning, you can even grow your nest egg even while you're receiving a guaranteed income.

It's important to look down the road, ten, twenty, or thirty years when planning for retirement. Using the right approach will ensure that your money outlives you. We plan for the day-to-day, but we also plan for the future, whatever it brings.

Planning your best retirement means utilizing various instruments and strategies to protect you and your wealth. You may feel comfortable with some risks, and that may include the stock market. Utilizing IUL's and indexed annuities can reduce risk and grow your wealth while helping you live out your dreams. Diversity in investments mitigates risks and improves financial stability.

If your retirement plan is too rigid, you lose the ability to be nimble and respond to the unexpected things life can bring. It's like running down the field with your nest egg. Maintaining your financial equilibrium and flexibility will keep you on your feet and allow you to outmaneuver trouble. It's the equivalent of being like the great Barry Sanders of the Detroit Lions was in football, avoiding opponents with quickness and speed. With a rigid approach, you might not be fast enough to sidestep, and you could get hit hard by unexpected events.

Some outstanding financial instruments are available today to make retirement all it can be while keeping your wealth safe and even growing it. I can help you with financial vehicles that provide a protected income value that allows you to withdraw a percentage of your account for life. With these instruments, you can still get increases in retirement, even AFTER you have spent all of your money!

Let's use a current product called a fixed indexed annuity as an example that uses various indices to determine what is credited to your account. The purpose of this product is to create a guaranteed retirement income that can also provide increases once distributions begin, all while protecting your principal against loss. As the index rises over time, your account value is credited based on how the index performs. However, you're Protected Income Value (PIV), what you base your income payment on, is typically credited with a higher percentage of what the index does. So, if the index did 10% and your account was credited 10%, your PIV could go up 15%! When you choose to begin income, your guaranteed lifetime income is based on a percentage of your PIV rather than your account value. Historically, the PIV could potentially be much higher than your account value. Plus, even if you deplete your account value, you still receive your guaranteed income, AND you will still receive increases if the index goes up in the future! If the index goes down, your principal is protected against loss due to poor market returns.

The safety net against unforeseen negative markets is what makes these types of products great. Risk is mitigated, and you're still set with guaranteed income that can increase in retirement, even if your account value is exhausted.

Some products even offer an initial bonus on the front end to your Protected Income Value. So, if you invest $100,000 with a company offering a 10% bonus, you'll automatically have $110,000 of PIV value even though the account is value is $100,000! If the index goes up over the crediting period, the percentage gain on your PIV starts from $110,000 rather than $100,000.

Other aspects of these vehicles are extremely attractive. Should you require long term care, your guaranteed income will double up until your account value is depleted, but even after that, your normal guaranteed income continues, with increases if the index has gains, until death.

I can help you find the right vehicle designed for you and your needs that will grow wealth, provide guaranteed income, and peace of mind. Working together, we can find sound solutions to your retirement needs so that you don't outlive your money. In fact, I have a proprietary process that will help you avoid the downdrafts and the unexpected storms that could blow your financial roof off.

If you're ready to change how you think and plan about retirement, then let's get started. I'll like to introduce you to a new way to plan for your retirement! We'll kick it off in the next chapter!

CHAPTER 5

The Mitch Lyons Wealth System: Retirement of Steel

To get anywhere in life, you must have a plan, and you must follow through with that plan. The financial hardships my family faced during my childhood were tough at times and certainly impacted my thinking. I knew that getting out of that situation was going to be left to me. In my mind, there was no way I was going to stay within the throes of economic distress. Due to my family's financial situation, I realized early in life that if I were to go to college, I would need to get a scholarship.

With the goal of getting a scholarship, I set my sights on the individual steps that would get me there. I had to work hard in sports and at school. Achieving any goal requires discipline. So, I made sure that I used a disciplined approach even as a kid. Attaining a scholarship for college was a finite thing. I only had so many years to achieve that goal and couldn't afford to waste time or veer from my plan.

Ultimately, I achieved my goal!

In many ways, I exceeded my expectations. Even though I got the scholarship, I had to restructure my plan to get through college and then make it to pro football. You can't grow complacent when goals are at stake. That's certainly true when it comes to building your wealth.

Putting off things for tomorrow or down the road just doesn't work. Having lived through the fallout of financial strife, it was important to me for my family to never go through that. After the career-ending injury in the NFL, it was time for me to move on. I could have gone into various kinds of businesses, but the one thing that drew my attention and ignited my passion was financial advising.

Helping people to build their wealth and to protect that wealth was my driving ambition. It still is. When someone follows your advice and puts money into specific products or other investments, you want to be certain that their money is safe. I made that my cardinal rule, and I follow it each day.

People place their trust in me to help them achieve their financial goals. Together, we build a solid financial future, one that my clients can count on in good times and bad. Making sure your money is safe and growing your wealth is my top priority. I want you to sleep well at night, knowing that your future is rock solid. Surprises, especially financial ones, are unwelcome.

> While we can't predict what will happen in the future, we can put your money in a viable and trusted product that will weather adversity and unexpected events.

We've had a strong dose of the unexpected recently. If your money is not protected from the unforeseen, now is the time to make some changes.

Going through the bursting of the dot.com bubble and the rough years that followed solidified my desire to change the status quo. I knew that to build wealth, I also had to build an impregnable fortress to protect my money.

Following the 2008 crash, it was painfully obvious to me that I needed to create my own path that would lead to financial success. If I wanted to remain as a financial advisor, and I did, it was essential for me to develop a new plan for my clients that was outside the box and totally secure. I don't know about you, but I got sick and tired of the stock market ups and downs and the unpredictability of it all. You probably feel the same way.

> Historically, if we look at how the stock market has performed, you might be surprised that overall performance was mediocre.

Did you know that 95 percent of wealth managers do not beat the market in any given year?

Charging people a fee of 2-3% to have their money underperform is not what I'm about. I can't stand it. I hate to see my clients lose money, whether to fees, taxes, or market performance.

The way to stop that is to educate my clients and help them move their money out of harm's way.

I've been a financial advisor for a long time. I know that human emotions can also come into play. People may be unhappy with how their investments perform in markets. Many people took a significant hit during the Covid-19 crisis. Money lost is money lost. Losing money is never a good thing.

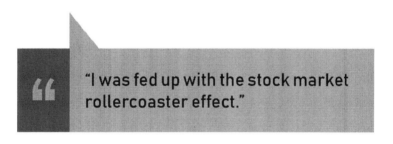

"I was fed up with the stock market rollercoaster effect."

It's never fun, and it can take years to break even. In essence, if you've got all or part of your money in the market, you're exposed. You're placed at the mercy of outside forces like a pandemic or financial crisis. You have no control, but *you* certainly have *all* the risk.

I was done with all that and said goodbye to the rollercoaster ride. I don't want my clients to take that ride either. Knowing what I know now about different vehicles to grow wealth, I'm positive that wealth can grow without the ups and downs of the rollercoaster and without the risk.

A great misconception exists that proposes you must have great returns to build wealth. That's simply not the case.

> **Putting yourself in the position to get great returns, also places you in the position to suffer great losses.**

You're putting your money at risk when there is no reason to do that.

A strong argument may be made that you can reach your financial goals and build your wealth by being a tortoise and not a hare. The slow but sure approach of the tortoise ultimately wins the financial race.

The hare's approach can be all over the place, up, down, and finally out. There are plenty of hares running and jumping from one investment to another. They get hit with losses and jump from one hot stock tip or mutual fund to another, not realizing that they may lose big again. They're hurried investors trusting the market may bounce back.

You may ask, "But didn't the markets do really well?"

When my clients ask me about that, I ask them in return,

"How do you think the S&P did the last 20 years?"

They answer, "Ten or twelve percent or so."

I then tell my clients, pandemic excluded, that the market has just come off one of its strongest bull markets in history, and the return was not 10 percent, but *six* percent from 2000-2019!

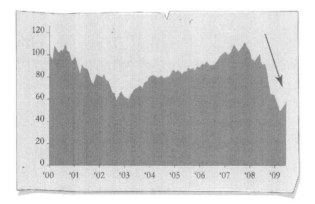

During the period of 2000 to 2009 ("the lost decade"), the S&P returned negative 1% annualized! If you were in that market at the time, that's what you made, but you also had fees that would have REDUCED your return (or actually INCREASED your loss!) even further!

Is that the phenomenal growth *you* expected from the market?

It is possible for you to grow your wealth safely and securely with a strong return. During that same negative period, index strategies worked extremely well, showing a 4.8 percent return. The world was in an economic slump, but index strategies performed positively.[15]

You can keep some money in the market, but a sound strategy is to diversify and move the bulk of your money to higher ground using a secure product.

Since we're living in unpredictable times, having your money grow predictably during retirement and guaranteeing you a tax-free income makes the most sense. Of course, it's up to you to decide how much of your wealth you want to put at risk.

---

15   The Worst Decade in S&P History; Facing a Less Favorable Market

Think of this, though:

> **Wouldn't it be great to get guaranteed tax-free income and still get pay raises? It's possible!**

First, we IDENTIFY exactly where you are and figure out the best road to get you to where you want to be financially. We'll break it all down and find the right vehicle for you. Financial planning is subjective. Each investor is different, and each retirement plan should fit the individual investor.

The Mitch Lyons Wealth System helps you discover where you are at any given moment on your financial timeline. Spotting your exact location, I can give you recommendations to help grow your wealth with a tailor-made approach.

> **Using this system, you can create a Retirement of Steel rather a retirement built from straw.**

Next, we FORTIFY your position by protecting what you have. I want you to be able to put your head on your pillow at night and not worry about your money. Placing your money into the proper, safe product is my goal. That way, we will both sleep well!

Once we've identified your position and goals, and fortified your current assets, we then ACCELERATE your retirement plan by utilizing strategies to maximize your after-tax retirement income.

Whether we're using indexed annuities or IULs to get the job done, we can mitigate your tax while growing your wealth! We can build an income stream that you will not outlive! Incorporating the Mitch Lyons Wealth System will find your retirement headed toward the promised land, a secure, safe place built on rock-solid investments. Building a financial plan on an unpredictable market and relying on simple interest is like building on sand. It leaves you open to shifting and settling that will ultimately weaken your financial foundation and keep you up at night. The Mitch Lyons Wealth System results in a RETIREMENT OF STEEL!

My system shows you how to build a properly structured plan with a sound foundation assuring you that it is capable of lasting generations. Therefore, you're not only protecting and growing your personal wealth, but you may also build a financial legacy for your children and your grandchildren.

Yes, the financial Promised Land is a real place. I know. I've been there, and I will give you the map and the ability to get you and your family there. You'll even enjoy the journey!

When things go well financially, and we have nothing but sunny skies, the difficulties of a time like the 2008 recession may fade from memory. Unfortunately, the *lessons* we learned during the storm fade from memory as well. However, when we get a less than subtle reminder, as we have seen recently with the impact of Covid-19, sunny skies can grow dark, and financial storms arise, seemingly out of nowhere.

Wouldn't you want to weather any financial storm in a properly structured environment impervious to the elements?

Sure, you would!

Using the strategies in my system, you can build a formidable defense capable of withstanding the biggest blows and still grow your wealth. You CAN have a

Retirement of Steel! Together we can build the retirement of your dreams, but we must work hand in hand. It's a team effort. I can coach you, motivate you, and get your financial position strengthened so it will outlive you. Working together is key.

The more I know about your goals, your dreams, and your current financial status, the more accurately we can detail the plan for your retirement.

We can't put off building wealth and formulating a retirement plan. Life moves too quickly, and before you know it, retirement is upon you!

Some financial planners rarely appear on your radar. They may check in with you now and then. Perhaps they'll buy you bagels, and you can talk about your 401k once a year. Being that removed from the client makes it difficult to know the client's current needs. With that kind of an aloof approach, a client's financial education may be poor or no longer relevant.

My approach is different. I want you to know exactly what you're looking at in time, distance, and money. You can't build wealth without knowledge, and being left out of the education loop will only hurt you. How can you make sound decisions without all the information you need at your disposal? You can't!

Bagels are great, but knowledge is better. It's power!

I can help you fast forward and get a real glimpse of what your retirement will look like. You'll know where you stand and what your options for protection and growth are. You know your potential! I'll give you the information you need to come back to the present and plan the right path for your wealth. This Time Machine will open your eyes. You'll know if your current plan will work, and you'll also see how the Retirement of Steel plan works.

We'll look at various scenarios, so you'll get an exceptionally good idea of what your options are. Retirement is a marathon, not a sprint. Let's build up those financial muscles to get the job done!

Considering critical and long-term care, catastrophic illness, and other unforeseen crises, we can make sure you're covered. In times of severe illness, you can potentially double your retirement income with this plan and/or have a lump sum available to help you manage a health crisis. Imagine not worrying about finances when you're battling a serious health issue!

Planning for the potential of a serious health issue may not seem essential when you're in your thirties or forties, but as you get older, health issues do arrive. Even younger investors have found the need for plans to assist them during times of financial and physical upheaval.

The right vehicles can act like Swiss Army knives, with each blade representing a different financial need like market protection, tax-free income, critical and long-term care protection, etc. Filling your financial bucket with money can be done, but it's much better for you and your family to fill it with tax-free money! Think of the possibilities!

By going the IUL route versus the 401k path, you can grow your wealth without the IRS sharing in your retirement harvest! Indexed annuities can protect the dollars you already have trapped in 401ks or IRAs. Why limit your potential when you don't have to?

Why would you stay in a plan that will ultimately be taxed at higher levels when you could have your retirement income tax-free and guaranteed?

Unless you're planning on making less money, why not get the income to ensure your lifestyle now and in the future?

The Mitch Lyons Wealth System can build your retirement fortress and protect your wealth from worst-case scenarios! Most people don't delve into the depths of analysis to discovering the finer points of their retirement. They assume it will be there, but as to specifics, they're still in the dark. It's my job to work through the process with you, so you know exactly what you have, what you will have, and what your income will be regardless of future financial assaults.

How much is peace of mind worth to you?

I had a phone call recently from the wife of one of my college roommates. She's also a friend of mine. My old roommate became a doctor and is now in his mid-fifties. Both were quite concerned and nervous about the stock market and what to do about their funds. He's only got maybe ten years before retirement. Should the markets tank again, he won't have much time to recoup his losses. They were hoping to find something better. They're limited by fund restrictions on other accounts.

I told them about some tried and true products that provide growth, guarantees, and security with zero risk. I can help you with similar products that can help you build your wealth without risk and worry.

If you've had enough of the financial storms, then it's time to come in out of the rain and find the sunshine. You can build a Retirement of Steel, bulletproof, and structurally sound that provides guaranteed income without the risk! The Promised Land is just an email away. Shoot me an email at mitch@mitchlyonswealth. com. I'm here to help!

Don't let uncertain times rob you of your wealth and your peace of mind. There is a better way!

In the next chapter, you'll discover the difference between a wise and foolish investor. You may be surprised. You'll also learn about another key element in the Mitch Lyons Wealth System.

Rookie year in
Atlanta, 1993

Mitch Lyons Tight End,
MSU

Sideline conference with Coach Bill Cowher

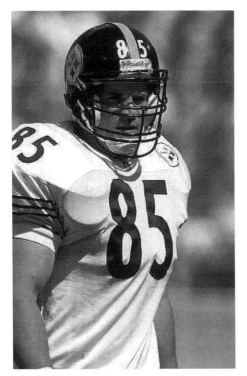

Pittsburgh
Steeler

The end
of the road

CHAPTER 6

Indexing: The Wise or Foolish Investor

Many things in life come down to whether we are foolish or wise. When planning for retirement, we need all the wisdom we can get. That truly should have been the case for me when I failed to pay attention to the writing on the wall.

I purchased a substantial amount of Qualcomm stock in 1998 when it was $5 to $7 per share. That was a wise decision! It was the top-performing stock on NASDAQ in 1999, and the stock jumped up to $200 per share over a year! I sold some shares on its ascent but then kicked myself when it doubled again! It was an amazing ride. The gains were fabulous. I could have reaped my reward, but I didn't want to pay taxes on the gains because it would have been substantial. I let it ride. The Dot.com Bubble kept expanding and then suddenly burst.

Well, I watched the stock tumble precipitously in March of 2000. Still, not wanting to pay tax on the gains, I continued to watch Qualcomm stock decline. I lost a lot of profits because I let the tail wag the dog. I finally did sell some of the stock, but it was painful. More than that, it was foolish.

Fortunately, I thought I had the luxury of time to make up for the lost gains.

I quickly found out in the Lost Decade from 2000 to 2009 that the road to wealth has significant hazards. In 2008, the road was for all intents and purposes, "Closed to Through Traffic." For me, it was like trying to run with the ball downfield and not finding any daylight because a massive wall of defensive players blocked the way. There was a solution to the problem, an alternate route I could have taken. But it didn't occur to me at the time.

If I had paid attention to the parable in the Bible about how a wise man builds his house on rock rather than the foolish man who builds his house on sand, I would have known that the huge sandcastle built by my Qualcomm stock and other investments would eventually wash away.

I made other foolish financial moves as well. I knew a guy who was well-established in the restaurant business. The gentleman had what I thought was a successful steakhouse. On the heels of his success, he wanted to open a new restaurant. I decided to go in as one of the investors. It looked logical to me because of what I perceived as his successful track record. With all the information I had, it seemed like the wise thing to do. Given the man's experience, how could the restaurant not succeed?

As it turned out, the restaurant failed to do well, and I had to kiss my investment goodbye. When you add up the painful lessons learned, it was an enormous wake-up call. I had to do better for my family and me, and also for my clients.

These scenarios bring up an important question.

> **Do you really want to invest in things in which you have no control?**

I had no control over how the restaurant did. I had no control over Qualcomm's performance nor the market itself. None. Having control of your money is pivotal in growing wealth. Relinquishing control puts someone else in the driver's seat, someone who is driving *your* money, and you have no idea if your money will arrive safely. As I think about it now, it was foolish to give up control. I regretted my decisions for quite a while, but I learned some valuable lessons from my folly.

However, I wish I had that money back where it could have been working for me the last 15-20 years. The thing is, and this is what I tell my clients, if you don't have your hands on the controls and the levers running the whole thing, you simply don't have control. There's nothing you can do. It's like being a blade of grass in the wind. You're totally at the mercy of the financial gusts. This is true whether the risk is company-specific, market-specific, or global.

> **Finding the right investments where you can keep your hands on the wheel is absolutely essential!**

Determined that I didn't want my clients to travel down the same dangerous road, I had to map out a new path that would lead them and me to wealth. I soon discovered, albeit too late to save my previous losses, that indexing was the incredible strategy that could drive us all safely to retirement.

Had I been wise, I would have moved my money into indexed based strategies like indexed annuities and indexed universal life (IUL) much sooner. I couldn't change the past or get a do-over, but I learned and embraced the advantages of indexing. Now, you can too!

You may not think that indexing has the sex appeal of picking stocks. Some people think it may not be trendy enough to talk about at cocktail parties. Then again, those conversations are rarely about how much you lose in the market but rather how much you gain. Lately, the cocktail party circuit has been quiet about stock performance with good reason.

Although indexed annuities and IULs don't have the glitz and glam factor, that doesn't mean that they're not viable solutions to building wealth, especially in volatile times. The thing is, if more people knew how amazing they are, the IULs and annuities would be talked up at every opportunity. It's all about how you look at it.

Using indexed products from insurance companies is the safe way to invest. The investments are protected through the insurance company mitigating your risk. Rather than investing directly into the stock market, your funds are placed in the insurance company's general account and managed by them.[16]

---

16   https://www.investopedia.com/articles/personal-finance/070215/pros-cons-indexed-universal-life-insurance.asp

Insurance companies manage billions of dollars. Those companies can tie your investment return to the performance of the S&P 500 index as well as other indices. Depending on the products, you may choose which indices you want. Insurance companies can buy options on the index your return is tied to on a much larger scale than you or I can as individual investors. This allows them to protect your investment from loss and still provide a large portion of the upside. It's done more economically that way, and then, of course, the insurance companies offer guarantees!

> **When was the last time you got a guarantee from your broker?**

Insurance indexing vehicles may have caps in place, depending on the product. The cap rates vary by product. They have upper limits attached to the returns over a specified period of time, typically a year or two. Indices also have a participation rate, which is the percentage of the index's return that the insurance company applies or credits to your cash value of the policy.

The bottom line is that you're transferring the risk to the insurance company, which is more than capable of handling it. Therefore, you have a floor of 0%. You have none of the risks and can reap the benefits if the index performs well. In a good year, you see gains. In a bad market year, you see no losses! None! With the ability to grow your wealth while mitigating the risk and taxes, indexing is a wise solution.

A broker can't promise you that.

Some people raise an eyebrow when first hearing about indexed products. They might think it's too good to be true. However, when I sit down with people and explain the reserve requirements insurance companies must adhere to and the scrutiny an insurance company is subjected to, people realize this is a viable option that should be considered.

Banks have FDIC reserves, but insurance companies are required to have much higher reserves. Additionally, many of the companies I work with have been around for over one hundred years. They've been tested by world wars, recessions, depressions, and the like and are still solvent. Going over the specifics of the financials with clients puts them at ease, and they gain a better understanding of how the products work. I put my own money into insurance-based indexed products, and I know they are viable and safe.

If you've invested in the market, you're probably familiar with brokerage fees being deducted from your account regardless of whether it gains or loses value. With indexed strategies, you may receive a slightly lower percentage than the index, but there are typically no additional fees. In other words, you're giving up a bit of the upside, but you're also insulating yourself from the downside. You are giving up something to get something, but risk is REMOVED from the equation.

As far as the method of determining the credited rate and the period over which it is determined, the insurance companies offer different options. You can pick the strategy that best fits your needs. For instance, I use a laddered approach. I have some money in the 1-year strategy, some in a 2-year strategy, and other funds for longer strategies. Varying the crediting time periods of your index selections can help diversify and smooth out your returns.

As we've seen over the past twenty years, things can go well or badly. Being flexible with your investments keeps you ahead of the curve.

RETURN RATES

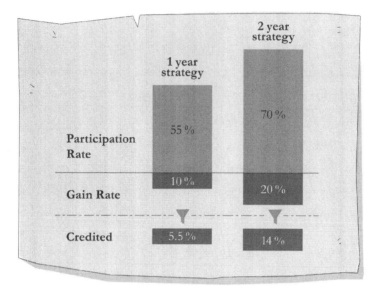

With other investments, there are accompanying risks, but not with this one. In a worst-case scenario, you're not going to lose 30 or 40 percent in a market crash. The worst you'll see is 0 percent gain, with your money safe and sound! Every time you are credited with a gain, that amount is locked in, and you cannot lose it to poor market performance going forward. Literally, you will not lose a dime. Knowing that, which investment vehicle do you want to include in your portfolio?

Over the years, I've seen people use an all or nothing approach to investing. They sock all their money into one or two fashionable stocks hoping for a killing. They're betting their futures and their retirement. They're hoping for the best, but hope is NOT a plan! Investors with that mindset are gambling on a stock to perform meteorically. As we've seen, that's laden with risks. That's not a retirement plan. It's a recipe for disaster!

Today, no one can afford a disastrous plan when it comes to retirement.

Having a more principled plan, one where you're not taking on unnecessary risk, is the plan of the Wise Investor. It's a prudent plan where you will not be wiped out by treacherous financial storms, even in the worst-case scenario.

TYPES OF INDICES

I walk my clients through the various types of indices that companies offer. Terms can vary a bit between companies. I cover all that during the planning stages to find the index best suited for my clients. Whether it's custom indices designed by well-known financial companies like Bloomberg or PIMCO, or a myriad of other indices, we can find one that can meet your needs. Many of the products are tied to the S&P 500 index. People are familiar with that index, and they have an understanding that it represents the 500 largest companies in the U.S. No matter what vehicle is, I make sure that you have the information you need to make the best decision for your portfolio.

By investing in insurance-based indexed products, you have the assurance that in volatile times, the company has you positioned to protect your investment. Regardless, your principal is safe! Historically, even in down markets, these investments still result in positive returns! You don't want a string of 0 percent years. So, we find the right vehicle for growth with the flexibility and the nimbleness to achieve positive returns while avoiding losses altogether.

Indexed Annuities Vs Indexed Universal Life

Both Indexed Annuities and Indexed Universal Life are insurance company products designed for retirement planning and protection. The IUL offers tax-free accumulation, tax-free distributions (through policy loans), and tax-free death benefits, along with the flexibility to alter your contributions.

Indexed annuities are valuable planning tools for a variety of reasons. You can invest in an indexed annuity with as little as $10,000. Annuities can provide tax-deferred growth, guaranteed income, and principal protection. There is generally not a limit as to the amount you can invest. I wouldn't recommend putting all your assets into an annuity. Each investor and situation are different. It is possible to construct the right plan for each person by discussing and understanding their unique situation.

It's important to know the accessibility of your money when investing in an indexed annuity. Typically, an indexed annuity will have a 5-10-year surrender period. The surrender period is a commitment of time that the insurance company requires in order to offer the guarantees and benefits they provide. With most annuities, you can access up to 10% of your annuity value annually without being penalized.

It's important to note that I never recommend that my clients pull out 10% from their retirement fund on a regular basis, so typically, this 10% limitation isn't an issue. It's available in a time of crisis, but I recommend leaving an emergency fund outside of an indexed annuity for life's surprises.

> **Please remember, we don't put all of our retirement eggs in one basket.**

Liquidity is important with investments, and these products do provide some access but not complete access.

I recommend IULs for several reasons. We've already discussed their indexed approach and protection from negative markets, but other reasons stand out as well. First and foremost is the tax treatment of IULs. Tax-free growth and tax-free policy loans (we'll get into these later) allow for higher retirement income amounts than other strategies. Putting a portion of your portfolio into products like these can provide moderate, consistent returns and generate higher income.

If you're considering purchasing an IUL, it is best to do so before age 65. Above that age, these contracts don't perform as well as an accumulation tool due to not having enough time for the strategy to be optimal. (Although it's important to note that there are other valuable reasons to utilize life insurance above age 65) Yet, if you're in the 40-60-year-old range, you're still in your accumulation phase with higher incomes, which can be a real asset for the IUL.

Many people nearing 59.5 years typically have a lot of money tied up in taxable accounts, and they're reaching the age where they withdraw money without penalties from their 401k plans.[17]

Repositioning some of those funds into an IUL can be advantageous in protecting your wealth, mitigating taxes, and ensuring your guaranteed income with growth potential.

IULs are like having a durable umbrella to protect you from financial storms. There are additional benefits common to many IUL's today. For instance, they will also help protect you from catastrophic illness, accident, or long-term care issues that eat away at your retirement fund. You can access your death benefit PRIOR to death,

17   https://humaninterest.com/blog/understand-
ing-the-rules-for-401k-withdrawal-after-59-1-2/

to pay for issues like these. Brokerage accounts can't offer that. With the risk taken out of the equation, you're gaining extra benefits and protections that will not only alleviate worry and loss but also will foster growth.

In times of need, such as long-term care, the ancillary benefits IULs offer are invaluable. I believe that it's prudent to take advantage of these products and incorporate them into your portfolio. I have done this personally, and I sleep well having this extra protection.

Adding both an IUL and annuities to your portfolio are key components to a secure future. There's no reason you shouldn't have both. The more diversified you are, the more sound your retirement can be.

IULs have a distinct advantage compared to 401ks not only on the tax side but also in the flexibility of withdrawals. With IUL's, you aren't subject to the age 59 ½ restriction to access without the IRS 10% early withdrawal penalty. Also, Required Minimum Distributions (RMD's) at age 72 are not required, like in an IRA or 401(k).

For years, we've been told that 401(k)'s are the answer to building a retirement nest egg. If we put our money away tax-deferred, we can save on our current tax bill. Then, when we take it out in retirement, we'll pay less in tax because we'll be in a lower tax bracket. That makes perfect mathematical sense, right? The only problem with this logic is this — based on our current government spending levels and underfunding of programs like Social Security and Medicare, what are the chances that we won't be seeing significant tax increases in our future? Whether it's higher tax brackets, lower income levels that tax brackets start at, new taxes, or reduced deductions, our government must increase tax revenue to pay for its reckless spending. With that in mind, what sense does it make to defer taxes now to, potentially, pay higher amounts of tax later? It makes mathematical sense to move your funds into an IUL rather than continuing to fund your 401k. Granted, matching employer funds help, but in the end, the money is going to be taxed. If you're still in the accumulation phase, you may want to consider making the transition sooner rather than later. Taxes most certainly will go up. You don't want to pay higher taxes on your 401k money. I can show you the math, and you can decide for yourself.

IULs for younger investors are really a prime investment when there is plenty of time for growth. Whatever your situation is, there is an indexing product out there that can offer growth, protection, and guaranteed income.

I've got a client who is in his 40's and has a number of businesses. He has several IULs and uses loans from these policies to fund other opportunities. He has become his own banker thanks to these vehicles. Becoming your own banker is advantageous and wise. Indexing products give you a chance to do just that. Properly structuring an IUL or annuity will reap great benefits for you and your family. I'd be happy to help you to learn more about which indexed products will work best for your situation.

In the next chapter, you'll learn what is lurking out there to destroy your retirement and how to combat it!

CHAPTER 7

Ensure That Taxes Won't Destroy Your Retirement

I was a typical nineteen-year-old impervious to danger. I thought I would live forever. You know the feeling that comes with being young and sometimes stupid. Well, a friend of mine borrowed a Porsche from his boss. In turn, I borrowed it from my friend. Talk about a sweet ride!

It was the dream car of most guys. I invited a football buddy of mine to come with me for a ride. We had to squeeze ourselves into the car, but we were ready to go. I really wanted to see how fast that car was.

We went out on a winding country road, a road that was perfect for an ultra-sports car. I pressed the pedal to the metal as we whipped around the curves. I got it up to 120 miles per hour but didn't feel confident with the curves at that speed. So, I thought about another country road that had a straight two-mile stretch. How fast would the car go on a straightaway? It was downhill for the first mile. At the bottom of the hill was a cross-street. Anybody could have pulled onto the road while we zoomed by.

Well, it was an extraordinarily dangerous thing to do. The road had a gravel shoulder, and an animal could have run out in the road. Nevertheless, I took the Porsche up to 138 miles per hour!

I didn't think about what could have gone wrong. We both might have been killed. I didn't think about the fact that my parents and my friend's parents might have gotten that awful call from the police, the one that makes every parent shudder to think about. Nope, I never thought about the possible negative outcomes. I just wanted to see how fast the car would go. Fortunately, we lived to tell about it.

Today, I get chills thinking about it. We might have been picked up in pieces in the trees and along the road. It was by the grace of God that I lived to tell about it. Now, driving down that same road, I shake my head and wonder how I could have been so reckless. Needless to say, that story came in handy when talking to my kids about safe driving!

Sometimes things happen outside of our control. Sometimes we take risks that we shouldn't be taking. Navigating the retirement income road can be fraught with dangers that can pull us off our course and maybe even cause us to crash. However, it is possible to find safe passage by carefully constructing our retirement portfolios to provide an income on which we can count.

> **Taxes can make us veer from the road. We may find ourselves with a financial flat tire that can make it hard to steer.**

Mitigating taxes in retirement can alleviate stress, worry, and doubt, giving way to peace of mind.

Taxes can change quickly, and as we've discussed, they most likely will be higher in the coming years. In our current climate, I don't have much confidence that the IRS and Congress won't change a lot of the tax benefits we may currently enjoy, like the Roth IRA and 401k. We're in a time of flux, and the call for higher taxes to pay for the stimulus packages and other programs are getting louder. The government is going to have to do something.

The country has seen steady growth in the amount of money invested in 401ks. Currently, it is estimated that there are $4.8 trillion in assets in 401ks. [18]

---

18   https://www.cnbc.com/2017/01/04/a-brief-history-of-the-401k-which-changed-how-americans-retire.html
https://www.irs.gov/newsroom/401k-contribution-limit-increases-to-19500-for-2020-catch-up-limit-rises-to-6500

Depending on what happens in our country and the government's need to raise taxes, those assets may make a large target!

 I have more confidence in the Insurance Lobby and its influence on the Congress to keep favorable taxation on insurance products compared to what could happen with taxes on the Roth IRA or even the 401k.

The favorable status towards insurance products makes the IULs stand out. Additionally, 401k's and Roth IRA's have contribution limits, which reduce your ability to accumulate wealth. For instance, as of 2020, workers under the age of 50 can only put up to $19,500 a year into their 401k. [19]

When it comes time to withdraw that money — you guessed it — you pay taxes on the money.

Saving for retirement isn't restricted to insurance products. The tax-free income broadens their products' appeal and encourages growth.

---

19   https://www.forbes.com/sites/davidrae/2020/01/16/401k-for-2020/?sh=12def0907903

With taxes likely to increase, this is the right time to insulate some of your money from taxes. Without a doubt, the most troublesome tax of all is the income tax. Most people in this country have their retirement savings in 401ks and IRAs.

Now, consider this.

We live in an accumulation-based society. We work extremely hard to put money aside for retirement. Yet, the downside is, we never consider the distribution phase of retirement. Either it's not explained as it should be, or we are just too focused on making money for retirement.

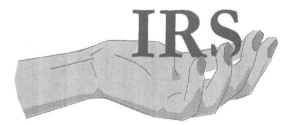

Unfortunately, we don't stop and think about the fact that the IRS will be waiting for us, palm extended more than ready to tax us on our income from 401ks and IRAs. In effect, the IRS is our partner in our retirement accounts!

The percentage the IRS may take could surprise you in a big way.

You should be equally prepared ahead of time and know just what the distribution phase entails and what your position will be. No one has a crystal ball, but it's safe to say that If you have money in a 401k or IRA, you may have a great deal less after the IRS gets through with it.

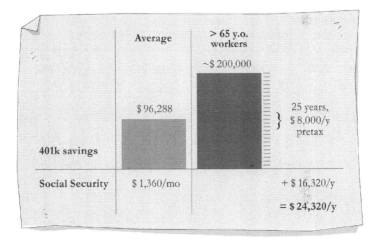

	Average	> 65 y.o. workers	
		~$ 200,000	
401k savings	$ 96,288		25 years, $ 8,000/y pretax
Social Security	$ 1,360/mo		+ $ 16,320/y
			= $ 24,320/y

Can you live on that?

While highly advantageous, IULs have received some bad press over the years. Unfortunately, some insurance agents haven't always structured IULs properly to benefit their clients and, consequently, they don't perform optimally. Brokerage houses jump on that bandwagon to entice clients to stick with the market, downplaying the risks, the fees, and the capital gains.

> A properly structured IUL, however, is a remarkable vehicle that offers growth protection and tax-mitigation.

I make sure that the products I structure for my clients are meticulously designed, ensuring them a retirement safe from danger with the benefit of tax-free growth and distributions. IULs can be the cornerstone of your Retirement of Steel! The IRS won't be waiting to swoop down and tax your income. You can rest assured that your money will be distributed every month tax-free.

Taxes and hidden fees that accompany brokerage accounts can be sizable. In good years, capital gains must be considered. Therefore, your bottom line is smaller. Peeling back the layers of the onion, you'll find money managers and advisors charging 2 or 3 percent, and even higher fees, on your accounts. Many people are unaware of the fees added on a yearly basis.

During the Covid-19 crisis, some people turned to their 401ks. While some people just withdrew their funds, others borrowed on the balance. At first blush, that money isn't taxable if it's taken as a loan. Nevertheless, if you don't pay the loan back, you will be taxed on the money. Further, if you're laid off or leave that job while the loan is outstanding, you will need to pay the tax on the unpaid balance.

I spell things out for my clients making, sure they are not surprised by things now or in the future. Building a bullet-proof retirement is what it's all about. I spend as much time as necessary to educate my clients about every aspect of the retirement process. You can't make sound decisions without having all the facts. It's your money, and staying informed will help you keep it.

I can't make decisions for you, but I can coach you and give you all the information you need. No matter what it takes or how long it takes, I make sure my clients are well-informed.

Paying attention to the issues surrounding the government stimulus package and the incredible spending that's going on, we know that money must be replenished. We can determine that taxes are going up either through a change of brackets and income amounts or through fewer deductions. Consequently, taxes are going to be an issue for everyone. It will be especially hard on retirees.

Since Social Security really can't be counted on, at least at the levels we currently see on our annual statements, it's necessary to fund your retirement with other vehicles.

Putting your money into a vehicle where you know it will eventually be taxed doesn't make sense under the current environment. It may make more sense for many people who are 59.5 years-old, to start the distribution phase on those taxable accounts. The tax rates are lower now than they are likely to be in the future. It's easy to forget that there are twists and turns and gravel on the shoulder as you speed down the road on your way to retirement. Spinning out and having your retirement income destroyed can happen. We can go back to the analogy of paying tax for the seed or paying tax on the harvest. It's best to pay tax on the seed and reap the harvest tax-free!

Another point to consider is that since the government has its hands in the 401k game, they could change the distribution requirements forcing people to withdraw their taxable funds much sooner or even on a regular basis. This way, the government doesn't wait for you to reach your distribution age, and they don't wait to get the tax money.

Estate taxes must also be considered. For the surviving spouse and children, this can be a huge burden. Placing your money in IULs assures that your family will not have to pay income taxes on the death benefits and will also escape estate taxes if the proper trust is included in the plan. Should your family own a business, the estate tax can come into play, often depleting working capital to meet the tax obligations.

Tax-loss strategies can help mitigate taxes on investments, but you must suffer a loss to write that off. Having to lose money to gain a tax benefit doesn't seem like a good strategy to me! It's far better to put your money in IULs, where you won't experience any losses. Some people use the loss to gain strategy as a reactive measure, but for me, it's a better, safer road if we take a proactive approach. So, why go the wrong way?

Within my client base, I'm noticing a migration of funds from taxable accounts to IULs. I coach my clients and educate them on the best way to build their wealth and develop a structure that creates tax-free income. Once my clients see the distinct advantages of moving their taxable funds to a safer vehicle that completely mitigates taxes, it's a no brainer. People wonder why they didn't reposition their money sooner.

Moving those hard-earned funds now is certainly better than waiting, especially when taxes may be substantially higher. Keeping that money in taxable accounts is like just giving away your money. The government will benefit, but not you!

Having been coached by some of the best coaches in the world, I'm quite familiar with their motivation techniques. Coach Bill Cowher of the Pittsburgh Steelers used to say, "You're either getting better, or you're getting worse!" His point was that you never stay the same relative to your competition. You go one way or the other.

Well, those wise words can be applied to retirement funding. It's either getting better, or it's getting worse. Strive to make things better, and they will get better. Slack off or not stay ahead of the tax curve, and things will get worse.

Many people suffered a financial fear about moving money during the Covid-19 crisis, thinking it's wise to just stand pat and do nothing. While the markets did come back from their pandemic lows, who's to say they won't plummet again in the aftermath of the pandemic?

So, what are we doing to make things better? Some people feel that sticking their heads in the sand is the safe thing to do. However, that exposes the bulk of your wealth, placing a large bullseye on your aspirations.

In football, broken plays can either be disastrous or miraculous. What at first appears to be a doomed play can suddenly turn into a touchdown. Keeping our financial plans moving forward is critical. To do that, we sometimes must react on the fly, just as in football. Look at your opportunities, and don't give up. Having facts at your fingertips, you can make things happen that are positive and will keep your retirement funds moving forward.

> **The biggest opponent of financial planning is the IRS.**

Yet, with the right game plan, you can be victorious!

Taking advantage of the tax code can be an advantageous strategy. I'm not a CPA or tax attorney, but you can consult one to learn more about these opportunities. However, the tax code changes often. A seemingly big opportunity may be non-existent in the next tax year. Keeping your antenna up and staying abreast of changes will give you lead time to make the necessary changes.

When the quarterback sees a defense that will thwart the play called in the huddle, he'll often call an audible and change the play to another that can exploit the defense. Tax laws are quite similar, and staying on top of the situation, you, your financial advisor, and tax advisor can make the appropriate call.

If you own your own business, there are several ways to mitigate taxes. Your CPA, tax attorney, and financial advisor can help you to do just that. Why not take advantage of legal remedies that will protect your income and wealth?

IULs are flexible products. You can move your money from one index to another to take advantage of developing situations. The overall flexibility within the IUL products allows you more breathing room and options that you won't find even in taxable accounts.

The non-taxable income from IULs will not affect your Social Security income like taxable retirement accounts can. You're much better off with income originating from non-taxable products. That way, your Social Security income will not be taxed.

Keeping the bulk of your money is the goal. Giving it away unnecessarily should be avoided.

A lot of people are working longer these days. They don't want to completely stop working because the cost of living is so high. Some may elect to receive Social Security benefits while still working. That can be a problem and result in higher taxes as well.

Retirement is also a time when people think of selling their homes or downsizing. If you opt to do that, make sure your CPA and your financial advisor are in the loop. People don't realize that real estate sales can have tax ramifications. I always promote talks with my clients and their CPAs or attorneys. This additional support keeps surprises at bay and allows us to plan for a more fruitful retirement while mitigating as much tax as possible.

The domino effect can come into play, and we don't want one move to knock the rest of the financial dominos down.

I've found that keeping the lines of communication open when it comes to my clients buying or selling assets saves a lot of distress down the road.

Just as you would have a yearly checkup with your physician to maintain your health, having an annual chat with your financial planner is good preventive financial medicine!

There are many competing voices out there who have various opinions about financial planning. When it comes to financial strategies, there are NO unbiased opinions. I admittedly am biased as well! I prefer to put my clients in financial strategies that can provide most of the market's upside but eliminate the downside. I go through all the possible options with clients so that they understand why I propose the solutions I do. If they find sources on the internet that say different, which is often the case, we start the conversation there and address those conflicting opinions. I'm not fond of surprises, and I don't want my clients surprised by anything.

Using the latest calculators and software, I walk my clients through the difference my solutions provide versus the alternatives. They can see what their money will do and its potential. Together, we can grow your wealth safely while not allowing market downturns and income taxes to destroy your retirement!

The essential thing I'm trying to achieve is to have an income that you can count on. How do you do that? You'll get all the ins and outs in the next chapter!

CHAPTER 8

Having an Income Plan You Can Count On

By now, you know I was a goal-oriented kid. I still am. Well, in high school, I wanted to be on the varsity football and basketball teams as a sophomore. I was driven to succeed. I practiced all summer long with the varsity basketball team, and I had one goal in mind. I had already achieved my first goal of playing varsity football that fall. I fully expected to be on the varsity basketball team as well that winter.

I thought my game had improved. Confidence grew, and I had high expectations to make the varsity squad. When the tryouts arrived, my confidence didn't wane. I did my best and felt sure the coach would pick me for the squad. He didn't!

It was a huge blow to my ego. I was incredulous. I thought, "Wait a minute! This isn't what I planned!" My spirits were low, and it took me a couple of weeks to work through the shock and disappointment. Was it my inability to play varsity basketball? I didn't think so.

I kept up with the varsity guys during the summer, honing my skills and getting better. Deep down, I felt that I wasn't being afforded the opportunity I deserved. My guess was that the coach felt that some of the seniors were owed the chance to see what they could do. Truly it seemed like a political decision to me because I felt that the best player should play . . . period. The coach ultimately decided to give them a shot first, so I was relegated to the junior varsity team. To me, it was, clearly, a defeat. My plans fell through, and I failed to reach my goal. I was extremely frustrated, and truthfully, embarrassed by the whole thing. I knew I could play at the level necessary to make varsity. It sure took the wind out of my sails. For two weeks, I went through a miserable existence. Yet, I played harder and kept pushing myself. I had to prove the coach was wrong. Caving in was not an option for me.

When you have the rug pulled out from under you, you can lose your bearings, and anger sets in. Fortunately, people doubting me has always fueled my desire to succeed.

Three games into the season, the varsity coach called me and asked me whether I was ready to move up to the varsity team! The older guys didn't play as expected, and so I was getting my shot! Ultimately, I attained my goal, albeit a few games later than planned! Determination and perseverance got me where I wanted to be. Staying there was another thing entirely!

I played well but ended up breaking my ankle a few games later and missed a chunk of games. I managed to get off the disabled list and return to action with a few games left in the regular season. In the playoffs, the team made it into the district finals! All those hours practicing during the summer paid off. It was a big deal, especially to my senior teammate, Steve Scheffler. It was his last season, and he wanted to make it through the state tournament. Unfortunately, Steve fouled out in the district final. I went in for him. If we didn't win, it would be Steve's last game. I remember he shook me and told me, "Come on, Mitchell! You can do it!" That was a lot of pressure, but I felt up to the task. Nobody wanted to go home. The game was close. With about one minute left on the clock, I missed the front end of a one and one free throw. A fellow sophomore had his shot at another one and one. He missed it on the front end too. That was it! We lost the game. Steve's plan fell through.

Although it was Steve's last high school game, his incredible work ethic, which he had demonstrated to me for years, paid off as he went on to be a Big Ten MVP at Purdue University, and later played nine seasons in the

NBA. He showed me that dreams can come true, and goals can be attained by having a solid plan.

Having a strong plan for your retirement income is imperative

However, that district final loss is an attestation to the fact that even with great intentions, hard work, and planning, sometimes things don't go as you plan. Finding the right income path to take for retirement does indeed call for careful planning and perseverance. If you do your homework, you'll find that there are ways to get guaranteed lifetime income.

You don't want to wonder in the middle of the night or during a crisis if your income will be there! Many people think that if they follow current trends that they will have the right income plan. That is not always the case. For instance, it's been suggested that the older you get, the more bonds you should have in your portfolio. Bonds can be advantageous — to a point. They can secure your principal and offer a reasonable interest rate. If you had the bulk of your portfolio in bonds, would it help your retirement income? They could, but there are other things you need to consider beyond the hype on TV and the internet.

> **Bonds may not be the best vehicle to have in your portfolio on a large scale.**

On the surface, people think investing in bonds is a safe alternative. Think again! Bonds can fall victim to rising interest rates. Should the markets go through volatile periods, bonds suffer, and so does your portfolio. Another warning sign for bonds is that they can be subjected to credit risk.[20]

What would happen to your bond investment if the issuers didn't meet their interest obligations or were unable to return the principal? Obviously, that's not an income to count on. Yet, people buy into the herd mentality that they need bonds and increase the number of bonds as they get older.

I disagree!

Just like my plan to make varsity hit a major stumbling block, taking the wind out of my sails, you don't want the bond market to take the wind out your financial sails!

---

20   https://finance.zacks.com/advantages-disadvantages-bonds-2350.html
https://www.fool.com/retirement/general/2015/06/21/3-retirement-crush-ing-unforeseen-circumstances-and.aspx

You'll go nowhere fast. In fact, without a constant source of wind, you'll be adrift and subject to the currents that may take you off course!

Like we mentioned before, and it's worth repeating, it's best to know what you're going to need for retirement income *before* you retire. Then we can reverse engineer your retirement plan to assist you in meeting your income goals. By taking a critical look at your income goals and evaluating your current investments, we can identify gaps in your income and work to fill those gaps.

A proper analysis helps you to avoid any nasty surprises. My high school football coach Dave Sukup always said, "If you fail to plan, you plan to fail!" The earlier you put your plan into motion is important if you're going to create your Retirement of Steel!

We start with a conversation to ascertain your current assets, annual contributions, age at which you want to retire, and your goals in retirement. Using a reasonable rate of return and the knowledge that accounts won't suffer from downdrafts in the market, we can establish your expected retirement income. If the income falls short of your needs, then you have time to change things.

You don't want to be adrift without wind or oars. Keeping forward momentum will help to grow your wealth. Since we don't know what taxes or inflation will be, it's wise to have several income buckets that will cover your expenses while still maintaining growth. Diversifying through IULs, annuities, and other investments will give you more options and flexibility.

> Knowing your long-term and short-term goals will also be a huge asset when determining your retirement income.

IULs, by their very nature, are long-term investments that will take care of you — and your principal is guaranteed against market loss. However, they are a long-term retirement strategy designed to optimize income 10-15 years down the road and beyond. In the early years of IULs, the numbers aren't as compelling. They have front-loaded costs. However, those costs decline going forward, and over longer periods of time, the annualized cost is a much lower percentage than what most people typically pay in a brokerage account or 401k. However, you get something for the value in the form of PRINCIPAL PROTECTION, LIFE INSURANCE, AND OTHER BENEFITS!

In looking at income flow in 15, 20, or more years, the numbers are also quite attractive relative to other investments. IULs are advantageous investments that are tax-efficient. Accompanied with growth potential, IULs provide income you can count on. I'm confident that IULs will outperform fixed interest rate investments like bonds or CD's going forward. However, IULs are just a part of your overall plan. You should have other financial buckets for shorter-term needs.

If you're looking for income in a mid-range timeframe like 5 or 10 years, a fixed indexed annuity may be the right vehicle. They certainly can outperform CDs while providing growth. Should a need arise where you need access to those funds, you can get that access, but not the entire balance. You can typically access 10 percent of the money in any given year without penalty. Just remember, it may be tempting, but it will diminish your nest egg quickly.

> **The best news about annuities is that they do better than CDs and have 0 percent downside.**

If you put that same amount of money into bonds, I don't think you will fare as well. It's all about eliminating risks, mitigating taxes, and optimizing your retirement income stream. Don't forget that bonds may decrease in value!

Safety and growth should be your top priorities. IULs, though, have other distinct advantages. Riders that come with the policy are numerous, and they can greatly benefit you and your family.

The Accelerated Death Benefit (ADB) features are extremely helpful if you contract a chronic or critical illness. You would have access to your death benefit, after certain terminal diagnoses, to help pay medical costs and other expenses so that your family will not be financially strapped.

As we explained in an earlier chapter, the costs associated with long-term care are quite high. Having this rider will ensure your needs are met while not ruining your family's finances.

There are a lot of other riders that can be added if appropriate.

The list of riders is lengthy, but you get the idea. You won't find these advantages with other investments like bonds; neither will you reap the security and guarantees. It's reassuring to know that some things like IULs are built to last in a volatile world.No two situations are exactly alike when it comes to retirement planning. By looking at the individual situation, we can put together the right products that will meet your needs now and in the future.

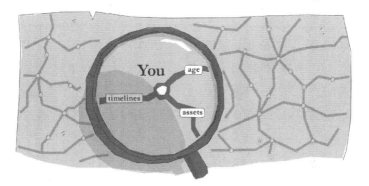

We look at timelines, assets, and age to customize a strategy that fits you. Wherever you are on the timeline, we can help build a secure retirement.

Some people have concerns that, due to health issues, they won't qualify for life insurance. Should you not qualify, there are some annuity products that can provide additional benefits at death. Since our health changes as we get older, the sooner you can get into the proper vehicle, the better.

> You'd be amazed at some of the newer products that offer Protected Income Value or PIV, which is actually higher than the account value!

It doesn't take long for that to happen. If death occurs, your beneficiary is given the choice of taking the account value as a lump sum or, they have taken the higher PIV value as long as they're willing to take it over a longer period of time. This could easily be a way to get a lot more money for your heirs. One insurance company will pay the PIV amount out over five years up to 250 percent of the account value!

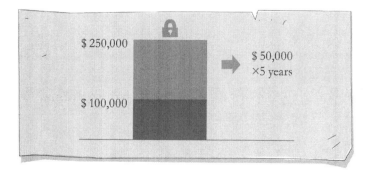

What are the threats in the world that can affect your retirement income?

> **Ridiculously low interest rates can be a threat as well as any tax hikes.**

We know taxes are not going away, nor are the tax rates going to be lowered. The earlier you get your money into the right vehicles, the sooner you'll be protected from any threats that can hurt your income.

We also don't know how politics may impact our retirement income. I feel more confident in placing my money into private contracts with insurance companies, especially with companies with a long track record that is trusted. Things can change dramatically from one day to the next, as we've seen. Putting money into the safest vehicle possible is the most secure thing you can do to protect your income and future.

Policy loan provisions associated with IULs are a major advantage of these contracts. In retirement, the insurance company loans you money with the policy value as collateral. By doing this, the money you receive is not taxable, and your entire account value stays invested, earning returns. Over time, your credited rate is likely to outperform the loan rate, enhancing your overall return.

> **There has never been a 15-year period that crediting rates have not outperformed loan rates!**

Knowing that and the advantages that go with IULs underscores the safety and growth potential of the product. Why not have growth and flexibility? Keeping your money working for you and not someone else is essential.

Getting all the information possible to help make sound decisions should be at the top of your retirement planning list. I had a couple a few weeks ago who came to see me. They are about five years out from retirement. We had some discussions about budgets, and they had some surprises.

As I walked them through a discussion on their monthly budget, the couple went back and forth about their needs. It's funny how and when people discover that they underestimated needs as they get closer to retirement. It can be an eye-opener.

The wife laid out the figures for her husband. She'd already gone through the numbers. When she showed him her figures, he said he agreed with the numbers except for one thing. He thought something was missing. She asked him what he thought was missing, perplexed at what she might have forgotten. He replied with a smirk, "About $2,000 per month!"

Adding about 10 percent for contingencies may be helpful. Knowing what income you will need to be comfortable in your retirement is imperative.

So, as I've highlighted throughout this book, there are numerous ways to ensure your income during retirement. There is another great strategy available that I would love to talk to you about it. It's a leveraged life plan that I'm using for myself as well as my clients who qualify. With something this good, it's hard not to be excited about it. The strategy is a five-payment retirement plan.

Basically, the client puts in half the total premium for only the first five years, and a bank puts in the other half for those five years. (The client does not apply for the loan. The policy is the sole collateral for the loan.) Then the bank pays the entire premium in years 6 through 10. With only five total payments, the client reaps tremendous rewards. You only contribute 25% of the total payment but earn interest on the entire amount, which is proven to outperform the loan rate over 15-year periods and beyond. So, the bank loan is repaid from the policy around year 15, and you keep the positive returns from the bank's money. This process will generally increase your retirement income relative to a self-funded plan between 60-100%. It's a unique product but may not be suited to everyone. However, if you qualify based on income or net worth, it's an extremely favorable vehicle that has been tested and proven to outperform self-funded policies.

I'd be happy to discuss these strategies and others that will fortify your income and give you peace of mind.

In the next chapter, we'll look at how you can be protected from the unknowns. Does that protection really exist? Let's find out!

CHAPTER 9

Protection from The Unknown

We all experience moments when we are blindsided by an event that forces us out of our complacency and routine, and something is altered in our lives, whether profoundly or to a lesser degree. Nevertheless, something changes. Often those changes make us reevaluate our position and take us in a new direction.

One thing is certain. We are changed forever by those events. They can be happy, sad, or catastrophic events that are burned into our memory. They are the kind of events that impact us, leaving a lasting impression on our minds. In fact, it's not uncommon to remember where we were and what we were doing when we were hit with bad news.

During the summer of my senior year in college, one such event hit me. Life was going along fine, and then suddenly, things changed. I had never experienced loss before in my life. My Aunt Suzy, who I was close with, had surgery to remove her one remaining kidney, which had failed. This procedure allowed her to get on a transplant list so that she wouldn't need dialysis any longer.

Although the surgery sounds like a big deal, it wasn't really considered to be out of the ordinary. The procedure wasn't expected to be life-threatening.

During the procedure, something went wrong. Apparently, while trying to remove her kidney, her bowel was nicked during the process. The problem was that the doctors didn't realize it. My aunt developed sepsis, an infection in her bloodstream. The immune system normally fights off infections in the body, but sepsis spreads throughout the body and can overwhelm it. For about a month, my aunt fought the battle but ultimately passed away.

It was quite a shock to me. I felt like I had gotten punched in the gut. We are all diminished by the death of a loved one. Her passing was truly heartbreaking. Unfortunately, I was hit by another unknown early in the fall of that same year.

The day after my third football game at Michigan State my senior year, my paternal grandfather died. It was so unexpected. Truth be known, even when death *is* expected, it still packs a wallop. Since it was so unexpected, I was greatly impacted by his death.

That time in my life was particularly uncertain. I didn't know what my future held. I hoped to play in the NFL, but I had no idea what would happen. I had the senior jitters anyway. You know the kind. You get that anxiety and the strange feeling in the pit of your stomach when you realize that in a few short months, you'll be out in the world on your own. It was a transitional time for me with a lot of uncertainty.

Not having experienced any loss in my life until that year and to be hit with two unexpected losses within such a short time was a tough experience.

Already unsettled, the unexpected deaths of my loved ones sent me reeling a bit. Life is like that, though.

> As we go through life and especially as people get older, massive changes can happen.

It's all part of the journey from birth until death. Life is filled with unknowns.

It is what we do to prepare ourselves for those unknowns that count. The mysterious nature of the unknowns, their unpredictability, and timing can make planning ahead difficult. Of course, we know death comes for us all inevitably, but other unnerving surprises can suddenly materialize in our lives. We can get gut-punched and thrown for a loop.

With the deaths of my aunt and grandpa, the clouds of uncertainty grew. I began to question a lot of things, and those questions, for which I didn't have ready answers, added fuel to the fire of my restlessness. Up until that time, my whole life had been predicated on sports. I was hyper-focused and driven to succeed in sports. I was on the path I always wanted. The losses I went through my senior year made me realize that something was missing.

I went through the NFL draft with trepidation. Finally, the Atlanta Falcons drafted me, and I was on my way to fulfilling my dream! I ultimately made the team, and yet there was still an emptiness in my life and anxiety. I had achieved my dream, but something was still missing.

During the early part of my rookie year, through some guidance from important people that God had put in my life along my journey, I committed my life to Jesus Christ, and things changed. However, I never forgot about the unexpected things that life brings. My faith, though, helped me through all the rough times that followed.

Having learned some big lessons personally and financially, I wanted to help my clients with the unknowns in their lives. When the unknown hits, something new to us, we often don't know how to handle it. We seek advice from people who have lived through similar experiences. I wanted to be that guy for my clients, a lighthouse in the storm, so to speak.

> **Going into retirement, it's kind of like heading into your rookie year or your first year in college.**

You only have a vague idea of what to expect. Thoughts of stability, security, and the future are charged with anxiety about the unknowns. You're sailing in uncharted waters. Sure, you may know east from west and north from south, but you don't know about the winds, the currents, and rocks near the shore. It can lead to anxiety and nerves.

Many of us can freeze under those conditions. Still, we must do what we can to prepare ourselves and our portfolios for the unknowns and the unexpected things in life. They do have a way of showing up. Therefore, there are a couple of things we can do.

1. Expect the unexpected
2. Prepare for the future expecting the best, but also preparing for the worst.

When you have covered all your bases, life doesn't seem as daunting!

In many ways, retirement can be the best years of our lives. It can also be a time for surprises. Our health can become an issue, which in turn can lead to financial strain if we're not prepared. Eliminating risks at this period of our lives is essential for our overall well-being. Stress caused by money and anxiety can wreak havoc on our health.

As we've seen, the world situation can foment the fear of the unknown. Even so, you don't need to become frozen in place, afraid to make a move. Planning ahead and creating your Retirement of Steel will strengthen you financially and emotionally. You'll acquire a buoyancy that will keep you afloat amid high tides and storms.

How do you build a financial fortress?

1.) Fill your portfolio with solid investments that will work for you and not someone else.

2.) Mitigate the risks and taxes.

3.) Make sure you have some of your portfolio that will provide tax free income and riders for calamitous events.

4.) Having contingency investments and accounts for the unexpected will assist you during unforeseen occurrences.

Completely sheltering yourself or your family is nearly impossible, but you can set up a portfolio that will give you the most shelter available. Having early access to a death benefit can alleviate several issues that arise during catastrophic illness or accident. Your spouse and your family will be taken care of. You'll also be able to cover the unexpected expenses that can rain down on you in tough times.

By properly structuring an IUL, you can have tax-free income as well as riders for the unknown and often costly events of life.

Let's look at some things you may not be expecting.

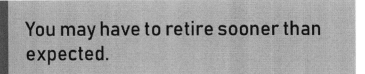

You may have to retire sooner than expected.

During your working years, you may fully believe you'll retire at 66 or 70, but things may change that. Companies have been shutting down due to the Covid-19 crisis. Other companies are laying people off to keep their doors open. Further, as we get older, we may become a liability to our employers. If employers are looking to cut costs during a financial drought, they may strongly suggest that their more senior employees retire early.[21]

---

21   https://www.forbes.com/sites/davidrae/2020/04/22/forced-to-re-tire-early-coronavirus/?sh=fcbfb1724662

Are you ready for that? Ready or not, this can be a big, unexpected blow. Looking at what you're bringing in each month and paying out will help you to meet the unexpected head-on.

Having money put aside in IULs will certainly help and will keep you ahead of the curve. You may not expect to retire early, and you may not expect the necessity to find another job just to make ends meet. I can help you mitigate those issues and find the product that's perfect for your situation. Neither you nor I can predict the future, but we can do a great job in protecting you from the unknown by working together. You can make sure that you have access to your funds, no matter what. You also have the potential for your money to keep working even during trying times while still taking care of your immediate needs.

As I get older and as my parents get older, I see health changes that can come out of nowhere. I have a friend who just turned 50. He never had health issues and looked fine. Hitting the big 5-0, his doctor suggested a routine colonoscopy to make sure everything was all right.

It turns out things were not all right. This guy takes care of himself. He eats right, and he's not overweight. He exercises and doesn't drink to excess. Yet, he's now on chemotherapy. No one, including my friend, saw that coming. Unexpected things that occur can make us feel like we're losing control of our lives. Although, if we have guaranteed fixed incomes, we do have control over our finances. During times of crisis, that is a big help in seeing us through exceedingly difficult situations. Should you lose money in the market with some of your investments, you can rest assured that your guaranteed income will be there for you. It's like having football pads on. You may get tackled, but you and your money are protected.

You have no control over how long you will live or if you'll be healthy. You can actively do all you can to maintain your health both financially and physically.

The long-term care, catastrophic illness, and other riders can be added to your IULs, often without charge. You're not just buying a life insurance product; you're also getting extraordinary benefits and invaluable peace of mind.

Talking to my clients about the advantages of IULs and their benefits, they see just how beneficial the products are. Using IULs in your portfolio keeps you proactive and in the game. You don't have the risks of getting sidelined, no matter what is thrown at you. None of us is impervious to the hazards of life, but we can mitigate the risks and eliminate worry and fear.

Building your wealth with high-grade financial steel is a game-changer. With enough money set aside, you will have the resources to do the things you want to do during retirement. Your transition into retirement will be much more positive.

It's important during retirement to keep active. Get out and volunteer or take a part-time job. According to the Motley Fool, they suggest not being the first in your social circle to retire.[22]

Obviously, in football, we build up our bodies and stamina to better take a hit and still get up and continue to play. Retirement is no different. Just as in football, we know we're going to be subjected to all kinds of impacts. We don't know when or even if they'll happen, but we can prepare mentally and physically just knowing a hit is possible. In the case of retirement, being financially fit will help us to take a hit and not be afraid of it.

---

22   https://www.fool.com/retirement/2019/11/14/6-ways-to-avoid-getting-bored-in-retirement.aspx

Expect the unexpected, and you can brace yourself. That doesn't mean living in fear but rather building a foundation strong enough that it can withstand a seismic impact.

Things change in retirement. You may have new expenses and changes in your deductibles. The transitional time from a work environment where your employer handled all the deductions gives way to you handling the whole thing. For a while, you may need training wheels, but you'll get acclimated and learn to handle all the new stuff.

Without kids and fewer tax deductions, like interest on your mortgage, you may get hit with a tax bomb. Plan ahead. Make sure you can mitigate as much tax as legally possible. Tax-free income will help and will not impact the taxation on your Social Security payments. Many changes go with retirement, and I can help you with them. We can sit down and evaluate your situation and make sure that all the bases are covered.

We can also sit down with your accountant to determine the best road to follow. With fewer deductions, do you take a standard deduction instead of itemizing? Let's find out![23]

If it's time to sell your house, how will that work for your bottom line? Let's go over that early! Find out where you stand in retirement and what Social Security benefits your spouse will get should you die if you retire at 66 compared to 70 or 72.

Planning for retirement is a lot like being in the NFL. We look at the game films, and we see our mistakes and then correct them. Then we move on to the next game. We study, prepare, and construct the best game plan possible to win!

---

23   https://www.nerdwallet.com/blog/taxes/tax-deductions-cred-its-for-retirees/

The temptation may be there to stick your head in the sand, but if you meet things head-on and address all the possibilities early, you'll be in much better shape and able to enjoy your retirement.

When my aunt and granddad died, I saw the aftermath of their deaths. It's an uncertain and complicated time, a time when big decisions can be difficult. As a financial advisor, I know the importance of my clients having enough money put aside, a death benefit that will be enough to give some breathing room to grieve during times of loss. Acting in financial haste following a death isn't the best thing emotionally or financially. Preparing ahead of time to ensure that needs will be met is a gift that keeps giving after death. An unexpected death shouldn't be followed by even more surprises that catch you off-balance.

Whether it's death, unforeseen brokerage or other fees, taxes, or health issues, life is filled with unanticipated events. Staying financially flexible will keep you resilient and will protect your wealth.

After having gone through significant changes and loss in my life, I'm confident that by sharing my experience and showing you solutions designed to protect you from the unexpected, you'll be able to live a secure Retirement of Steel.

In the next chapter, we will look at the journey to retirement and the beautiful financial haven that can await you!

CHAPTER 10

The Power to Control Your Retirement

When I left Atlanta and signed with the Pittsburgh Steelers in April of 1997, I didn't know much about Pittsburgh or the people. I was familiar with the Steelers' great Super Bowl teams of the 70s (my MSU Coach George Perles had been a member of the coaching staff for all four Super Bowl wins back then). I also knew that Pittsburgh had been a blue-collar steel town during that time.

What I came to find out was that the Rooney family, who had owned the franchise since 1933 when patriarch Art Rooney bought it, was deeply rooted in Pittsburgh. They exemplified the people of Pittsburgh-tough, hardworking, resilient, and loyal. Pittsburghers had gone through tough economic times with the downturn of the steel industry in the 1970s and 80s. Up to that point, the Steelers had only had two coaches since 1969 - the legendary Chuck Noll and Bill Cowher. Both of those coaches embodied the principles of the people of Pittsburgh, and their teams took on those same characteristics. Steeler teams embodied the toughness of the Pittsburgh people with their famous logo representing the three materials to produce steel — coal, iron ore, and steel scrap.

Coach Cowher always talked about keeping a level head no matter the circumstances, winning or losing. "You're never as good as they say you are, but you're never as bad as they say you are," was a saying he always used to keep us grounded. "Pack a lunch and bring a flashlight" was a saying Coach Perles had picked up in his Steeler days.

Winning was the result of doing all the little things correctly in practice and training so that they became second nature on game day. Unconscious competence was what we called it — reacting as you've been trained and not having to think about it.

Retirement is like a game on Sundays in the NFL. It's a culmination of an off-season's worth of work and a week's worth of fine-tuning specifically geared to that week's opponent. If you didn't do the work required leading up to the game, you could fully expect to fall short on Sunday.

The same is true of retirement.

If you haven't taken the time to carefully plan and account for all the different things that could happen on game day, you are positioning yourself to fail on the game day of retirement.

With all the changes we've seen in the world recently, there is no better time than now to plan properly for your retirement. Having a game plan in place increases your financial security and mitigates risks. Carefully planning your retirement must become your top priority to protect your future and your wealth.[24]

I'm a deliberate person who thinks things through things thoroughly before I make a move. After the 2008 crash, I knew I had to change my financial course and that of my clients. Life is too short to suffer catastrophic losses. I set out to find the best vehicles that would build a Retirement of Steel for my clients and myself.

I was the test case. If I could make it happen for me, I could help my clients secure their futures as well. Going over all the material and information I could find, I concluded that retirement planning had to be

---

24   https://www.lifehack.org/512533/why-retirement-planning-more-important-than-you-think

overhauled. The status quo just wasn't good enough to ensure my money would grow and be there for me when I retired. With the significant losses that tackled me in 2008, I was unwilling to place my future and that of my family in the hands of volatility and market fluctuations.

My clients deserved better vehicles to build their wealth. The more I learned about IULs, the more I knew I had found the right vehicle. It was no longer necessary to watch the stock ticker. Anxiety was no longer part of my financial planning. Even my clients, who took my advice, made it through the pandemic unscathed.

Let me tell you, it's absolutely vital to have your money in safe investments that will perform regardless of the stock market, world events, or whatever else may happen; and provide you a guaranteed tax-free income for the future. The vehicles must be bull-tough and able to withstand major hits without losing a dime. Building the Retirement of Steel for myself and my clients became my passion.

Don't build your financial house on the sand. Build a rock-solid foundation to account for life's ups and downs. Fortify that foundation and provide you and your family a Retirement of Steel - one that can handle anything life throws at you.

Don't trust "Conventional Wisdom."

Don't accept the status quo and keep doing things "the way we've always done it." There are better alternatives to accumulate and to distribute wealth than fee-based brokerage accounts or 401k plans that aren't protected from market downturns. Be willing to take a fresh look and understand how these strategies work and why they provide more income and protection. At the very least, educate yourself so that you can at least make an informed decision. Know what you're saying "NO" to!

The Retirement of Steel was a mindset I adopted while playing for the Pittsburgh Steelers under Bill Cowher. He often said that the "Toughest man in the world is a coward when he's tired." What he meant was that we needed to push past tired in our training so that we wouldn't get tired on game day; and ultimately, defeat a tough opponent by outlasting them. He urged us to have a spine of steel to handle the adversity that was sure to come in each game and season. We can plan for retirement much the same way by taking the necessary steps to ensure that we can handle anything that comes our way in retirement.

Market Protection

Increased Income

Tax Efficiency

My method is different because I question every concept we've been taught from a retirement planning standpoint. My strategies are not conventional; because they offer MARKET PROTECTION, INCREASED INCOME, and TAX EFFICIENCY.

Following my blueprint for a Retirement of Steel, you can grow your wealth significantly, and best of all, your wealth will never go backward. Losses are extinct.

> **Why work 30-40 years to have the bulk of your wealth stripped from you in one precipitous moment in the markets?**

You can do better. You *can* build an impenetrable Retirement of Steel!

In reflecting on my 55-year-old friend who suffered a catastrophic stroke, he didn't have the protections in place. He had everything in front of him. His future was all mapped out. He wasn't sick. He was successful and had a wonderful family, and then, BAM! I don't want that to happen to you! I don't want that to happen to anyone. The thing is, security is attainable, but you must move ahead to get it.

We've seen the writing on the wall from the history of the stock market to the pandemic. Things are volatile right now. We don't know when things will get better or what will cause the next market crash. Yet, I know you can build your wealth despite uncertain conditions. You can have a secure income even when times are bad.

Waiting for things to improve before making a move is a dangerous strategy, especially with today's economic climate.

After moving my money into IULs and annuities, I never looked back. The pandemic underscored that I made the right choice, and so did my clients who took my advice. We weathered the financial tidal wave. You can too!

I'm friends with a great group of guys. We get together frequently and discuss how we're doing and what we're up to. They asked me about my book and how it was going. I told them it was going well. One of the guys was in the middle of a job change, which meant taking a closer look at his 401k. I said, "Yeah, you know, we've all jammed money into 401ks with the hopes that we're going to be in a lower tax bracket in retirement." They looked at me, and I continued, "Does anybody think we're going to be in lower tax brackets later?"

"Oh, heck no," one guy said. Then across the board, all of them, "No! No way!"

I turned to them and said, "Then why in the world are we pouring money into a 401k?" They all looked at me, dumbfounded. They said, "Is that in your book?"

"YES, I'll get you a copy!"

All of them agreed that we need to have an in-depth conversation about their retirement plans.

It was kind of funny to see all their heads nodding up and down. Each agreed tax would be higher. "That being the case, why would *you* put your money in 401ks to likely be taxed at a higher rate later?" I really wanted to bring the point home.

The lightbulb came on. I could see it in their eyes. They got it!

I made another point. "If you're going to get a match from your employer, then take the match in the 401k. That would be smart, but don't put any money above the match in the account."

Suddenly, they're ready to talk about alternatives and how to build their wealth despite higher taxes! Come to think of it — I don't recall that many people tell me that taxes are going to go down! The moral of the story is that if you stick with status quo investing, higher taxes will probably go with it. Kissing your money goodbye is painful, but there is a preventative plan, and I'd be happy to show you how you can fortify and accelerate your wealth while mitigating taxes!

If you're fine with paying more taxes and having less income, an income that may not be guaranteed, I wish you well. Maybe you don't need to build your wealth and that things are fine the way they are. Maybe you can survive another major financial crisis. If you can, God bless you! That's great! But if you can't, let's talk! This is the right time to think outside the box.

You know that when you build a house and sink a lot of money into it, you don't use inferior materials. You buy the best materials you can find to ensure that your house isn't made of straw and subject to strong winds and storms.

All NFL teams want to win the Super Bowl. It's the ultimate goal. You can't go all the way to the Big Game with inferior players who don't have the skills to get the job done.

When the draft rolls around each year, the owners meet extensively with their staff and determine where they are weakest in terms of positions, whether it's offense or defense. Maybe they need a middle linebacker or a running back. They don't go into the draft with the idea they'll take a mediocre player prone to injuries. No, they go with the best they can get. You can't win without the best team. Retirement is no different!

People who have the mindset that they want to stay in stocks raise their eyebrows when I tell them that over the past 20 years, stocks saw a 6 percent rate of return. The person on the other side of the desk will say that they thought it was closer to 8 or 10 percent. My reply is that over the past 100 years, that was true but not in the last 20 years. Things change, shouldn't strategies? Flexibility is invaluable when building your retirement.

Going on preconceived notions and stale information is counter-productive when it comes to building your wealth. Ongoing analysis and education are paramount if you're going to stay ahead of the curve. Many people build their retirements more on automatic pilot rather than on careful study. If people work for a company that offers 401ks or pensions, they simply check the box and sign up for the plans. They think it's cool and don't do the deep dive when it comes to how things will shake down at retirement. Surprises about tax bills and fees may throw a sizable wrench into your retirement plan. Things evolve, and we must be willing to evolve with them.

As an example, I had a conversation with someone about portable 8-Track players. When they first came out, we thought they were awesome. We didn't mind that you'd be in the middle of a song, and then it would click over to another channel to finish the song. We got used to that. Now, compare that to streaming music today. Which would you prefer? Compare that to the IUL solution.

Once people understand the math behind an IUL, the distribution options with the policy loans, and when they look at the math and compare it to what they're currently doing, they see they're going to drive more income out of it. If they see 20 percent or 30 percent more income or whatever it might be, it's hard to ignore the math.

So, why would you keep listening to the 8-track when you can just stream music? You make the choice. Do you listen to the old way or the new? Well, do you want to grow your wealth securely or stay in dangerous waters?

The bottom line is we have a lot of uncertainty economically. We now wait to see how it will all shake out, the job losses, businesses going under, and entire industries destroyed. Who knows what the future holds?

If you add in an incredibly low-interest-rate environment, which basically renders bonds useless and highly dangerous, is that something you really want to count on? Should interest rate levels rise, and with taxes likely to increase in the future, it's a huge gamble.

I mentioned earlier that you spend 30 to 40 years saving for your retirement. Can you afford a major hit during retirement when you don't have the time to recoup your losses?

Moving into IULs and annuities can give you the protection you need as well as good growth. In the NFL, you can be running the ball to the end zone, but if you're stripped of the ball before you cross the goal line, all your effort was for naught. Retirement is the same way.

Building up your financial stamina is crucial to surviving retirement. In football, every team has conditioned players. Some are in better shape than others. The key to victory is to outlast the opposition. If you're building your financial muscles and able to outlast whatever is thrown at you, you will succeed in retirement.

Iron Mike Tyson was a tremendous fighter. He was great in the first three rounds. Normally, that was enough to put his opponent away. Tyson's fights rarely went the distance. Well, that was true until Buster Douglas showed up. Douglas was an underdog, and most observers expect him to be knocked out quickly by Iron Mike. Well, the fight went longer than expected. Douglas hung in there. Tyson got tired. One solid punch took Tyson out of the fight and cost him the heavyweight title. Don't get caught on the ropes without enough energy to finish the fight.

You must protect yourself and build that financial strength so that you won't get knocked out. Move your money into protected products that will help you today and in the future.

We commonly think that practice makes perfect. That isn't the case. Perfect practice makes perfect.

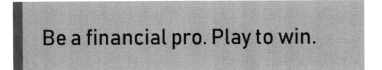

Be a financial pro. Play to win.

Under Bill Cowher, we practiced hard so that, by Sunday, we were more ready and in better shape than our opponents. You can't show up on game day expecting to win if you've had lazy practices.

You can't show up to retirement with a mediocre plan and soft training. Don't assume that your 401k will take care of you. Don't assume that your retirement is safe. No one knows what taxes will look like next year, let alone several years from now. Instead of taking the easy way out when you really should be preparing, do your homework. Find out where you stand today and in the future. Your family is counting on you.

I can help you to build your Retirement of Steel. I'm always available for my clients. Like a coach, I'll make sure you're ready for retirement. You'll be in the best financial condition to meet all that's thrown at you. You won't be alone.

Your money can be safe. It can outlive you. It can provide tax-free income and still have enough left over in death benefits for your loved ones. Let's talk about it, and let me show you how we can use the right tools to protect you from the unexpected, the financial hits, and economic uncertainty.

You've worked too long and too hard to let your money go unprotected. I've walked the walk before you. I know where you can find the Promised Land. Let's work together to build your Retirement of Steel today!